Online Video Revolution

Online Video Revolution

How to Reinvent and Market Your Business Using Video

John Cecil

palgrave
macmillan

First published in 2012 by
PALGRAVE MACMILLAN®
in the United States—a division of St. Martin's Press LLC,
175 Fifth Avenue, New York, NY 10010.

Where this book is distributed in the UK, Europe and the rest of the world,
this is by Palgrave Macmillan, a division of Macmillan Publishers Limited,
registered in England, company number 785998, of Houndmills,
Basingstoke, Hampshire RG21 6XS.

Palgrave Macmillan is the global academic imprint of the above companies
and has companies and representatives throughout the world.

Palgrave® and Macmillan® are registered trademarks in the United States,
the United Kingdom, Europe and other countries.

ISBN: 978–1–137–00307–2

Library of Congress Cataloging-in-Publication Data

Cecil, John.
     Online video revolution : how to reinvent and market your business
using video / John Cecil.
        p. cm.
     ISBN 978–1–137–00307–2
        1. Internet advertising. 2. Internet marketing. 3. Internet videos.
     I. Title.
HF6146.I58.C43 2012
658.8′72—dc23   2012022935

A catalogue record of the book is available from the British Library.

Design by Newgen Imaging Systems (P) Ltd., Chennai, India.

First edition: December 2012

10 9 8 7 6 5 4 3 2 1

Printed in the United States of America.

Lovingly dedicated to Britt and my kids, Jayden, Ella, and Jack.

Contents

Figures

Acknowledgments

S pecial thanks to Tim McHale, Taylor Carlson, and Belinda Sanders for helping me write this book. Thank you to my colleagues at Innovate Media: Dave Winters and Robert Ardell.

Special thanks to eMarketer—Crystal Gurin, Vice President/ Publisher and Clark Fredricksen, Marketing Communications Director for providing case studies, charts, and research for this book.

Introduction

This book is for you—a marketer who is turning to the use of online video to reinvent a business, website, or marketing campaign. Over the last few years the Internet has exploded with dramatic changes, especially in the area of video, including how it is used and where it appears. More online video is being viewed by Internet consumers to get information about products and make buying decisions.

The results have had a worldwide impact on online marketers and brand builders who have to work hard to maintain their visibility via an Internet presence. The sweeping changes that have occurred require that marketers quickly become savvy in the many areas that influence their marketing outcome: search engine ranking, pay-per-click advertising, radio or television advertising, content marketing, webinars, teleconferences, social media, and now video.

What was once a text-based Web has quickly evolved into Internet content that is now primarily video-based. Many tools are widely available to help create visibility on the Internet with video. These tools include how-to books for producing video content, and tips that guide you step by step using free or low-cost resources.

With the explosion of information moving quickly through the Internet every second of every day, it is critical that you have the undivided attention of those visiting your website. Video can, and does, increase a website's conversion rate of visitors to buyers.

The book you have in your hand will help you market your product or service effectively using video. I have been producing and delivering video over the Web for almost a decade now. I hope to pass on my experience and the things I have learned to you so your work will be easier, your success greater, and your profits explosive.

In this book you'll learn the following:

- ☑ Components of a marketing plan and where video fits into your plan;
- ☑ How to create a greater return on your video investment;
- ☑ Production issues to discuss before starting a project;
- ☑ Delivery options that can support your specific needs;
- ☑ How to use video with social marketing and search engine optimization;
- ☑ Why you'll need a delivery mechanism for your video;
- ☑ Why increasing your conversion rate is important to your ROI;
- ☑ How the web is turning from a text based medium to a video based medium;
- ☑ How to maintain your video plan;
- ☑ If you should think about video for your business;
- ☑ When you should use video for your business.

Using the information in this book will help you ensure that your video ultimately creates the highest possible return on your investment, which comes from converting your prospects into paying customers. Taking the steps I have outlined for you will move you to increasingly higher returns on your investment with the use of video content.

CHAPTER 1

Lights, Camera, Action! Text Goes to Video-Based Content

My excitement and passion for video goes back to my early career days. I was working at Yahoo! during the beginning years of the company. Technology was in its infancy, the Internet was still in the early stages of growth, and the ad environment was constantly changing. What we knew about the Internet, online marketing, and reaching customers was limited only by what our imaginations could dream up. We worked long and we worked hard. It was an exhilarating place to work.

Around 2001, I began planning my next career move. I looked at where I wanted to be in a few years and the changes that had occurred in technology during my work with Yahoo!, I knew that video was going to be a key component in the growth of the Internet. Video, from my perspective, was the latest and greatest shiny new object, and maybe it would create a 360-degree change in a text and graphic dominated environment.

Throughout history, technology has changed quickly. The Internet is an important example of how the human imagination combined with effort and energy can create something new. Think about it, even though the Internet is by all definitions "new" technology, as early as 2001 it had already added video and made it available 24 hours a day, every day of the week.

The purpose of the Internet has also shifted. Today, it has taken on a much more profit-focused orientation, commercializing information and selling products and services. In the past five years, businesses have finally begun to use this perfectly priced technology to their advantage to keep in touch with clients, draw in new customers, promote available products, and sell their services. You'll learn more in this chapter about the purposes of the Internet as it relates to video and how to use it as a powerful tool to increase your revenue, including the following:

- ☑ Understanding how we're transitioning to video will help prepare you to market with video;
- ☑ The surprising number of customers not watching video content;
- ☑ What content you can provide to your viewers;
- ☑ What customers will remember about your video message.

Words Shift to Pictures

Words are becoming less and less prevalent online. It was not long ago that the Internet was a place to turn to for written content much like an enormous invisible library in the sky. It was filled with pages and pages of personal experiences, how-to and self-help information, business guidance, fiction and nonfiction stories, forms, templates, and samples. Content was king. Businesses of all sizes were marketing themselves by placing written content on their websites or on sites that linked back to their own. Articles and newsletters were popular beginnings and were uploaded on a regular basis to a company's website in an effort to increase content. This written content also served to demonstrate the expertise of a company, product, service, or service provider, and helped buyers make decisions about purchases.

Articles and newsletters then became available to website visitors at no cost. These items were automatically made to show up in e-mail inboxes on a regular basis. Various delivery tools were used to make this happen. The price, oftentimes, was only an e-mail address provided by a consumer, customer, or interested prospect. The company receiving an e-mail address could then promote its future products and services to you, as a subscriber or member. Delivery of this content became an integral part of a balanced plan for online marketing.

Content delivery also supported brands and created name visibility for products and services. Customers were reached on a regular basis and they began to recognize company names, logos, or taglines in each e-mail that appeared. The same was happening with your own prospects, who received regular and consistent messages from you. And the price was right. For the most part, keeping in touch with customers on a regular basis via e-mail was, and still is, nearly free. After purchase of the initial hardware and software, custom messages can be sent in bulk for virtually no cost. This definitely beat the expense of sending out hard-copy direct-mail messages with real stamps on them. Potential customers were spending a lot of time in front of their computers reading your marketing messages, jokes, stories, and other learning materials. But it was all text-based delivery, and frankly it became hard to read all the information that appeared on-screen.

Then text and text-based products began to evolve into a visual experience, with video footage and video-based products on the Web. It was clear for some time that the landscape for promotion on the Internet by online marketers was changing. The fundamental changes were not evenly distributed across each industry, and the complications were universal. Because the primary medium of the Internet is shifting from text to video, with pictures that include graphics, color, movement, and action, communication methods are also required to change.

The Internet was not the first change we saw through technology. Broadcast radio and then television, after their introduction into the lives of Americans, provided entertainment, information, policies, perspectives, and product awareness delivered directly into households. Families gathered around these technologies, great for their time, and eagerly awaited messages that were only spoken words and simple images with which they could create pictures in their minds. Presidential messages, news, and mystery stories were delivered via radio and were well received by listeners. Eventually, television appeared in homes throughout the world and delivered these same messages with pictures. Television changed from black-and-white pictures with only spoken text, to full-color pictures, graphics, action, and music. The evolution continued, with televisions of all shapes and sizes available for purchase. Messages were broadcast by television to promote products and services available to viewers.

Viewers quickly became familiar with company and product names, logos, taglines, and easy-to-remember jingles and slogans.

Radio and television continue to exist even though video can now be easily viewed from any place throughout the world.

Video is yet another method that marketers have available to reach their customers, and it presents challenges to some and success to those that master it. "Online video is unlike any commodity in advertising right now," says Dave Otten, CEO of LongTail Video. "It's a medium that has transformed the Internet itself, propelling consumers to upgrade to higher-speed connections just so they can partake." The use of video is a must in the day-to-day business operations of any company wanting to create visibility or brand awareness. Everyone has an opinion. Everyone has a story. Everyone has a perspective, idea, thought, or comment. People are always willing to share these when asked. Video is available at all times and facilitates the task of recording feedback from others. This material was written to help you capture on video the information necessary to engage your prospective buyers. You may present them with facts, stories, statistics, information, or success stories. But your format will be video. Consumers are looking for fun action shots that deliver your message in an instant, not boring pages to peruse for your final pitch.

Video is an area in which you must possess great skill so that your company will prevail against your competitors. Your efforts as an online marketer promoting your product or service require you to skillfully use video to transform your prospects into paying customers. To promote your product or service on the Internet, as an online marketer, you need to know how to use video in dedicated marketing efforts. The more you know about this topic, the better your use of video during your campaigns, and the better you will be able to meet the viewing needs of your prospects.

When the switch over from text to video began, you may have been caught by surprise, like the majority of online marketers. You probably did not know how to handle this incredible shift. You could produce video. You could produce a television commercial. But you, like your colleagues, were probably at a great loss as to how to deliver information into your customers' hands. Ad agencies were skilled at getting their commercials seen by consumers. They had methods that were proven and reliable and had withstood the test of time. As for videos produced by online marketers to promote a product or service, getting these videos seen by consumers presented a problem. Primetime in 2002 was on television, not the Internet.

YouTube started the online video revolution, and you, the online marketer, will finish it. The transition began as text was used less and YouTube video footage was used more. Many changes have occurred with the placement of video content on YouTube's website, specifically the evolution of text to video.

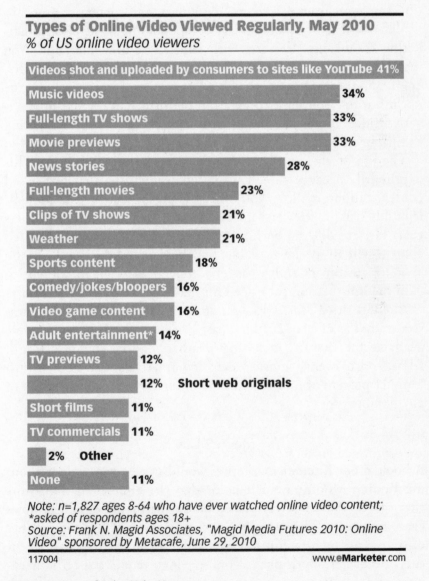

Types of Online Video Viewed Regularly, May 2010
% of US online video viewers

Videos shot and uploaded by consumers to sites like YouTube	41%
Music videos	34%
Full-length TV shows	33%
Movie previews	33%
News stories	28%
Full-length movies	23%
Clips of TV shows	21%
Weather	21%
Sports content	18%
Comedy/jokes/bloopers	16%
Video game content	16%
Adult entertainment*	14%
TV previews	12%
Short web originals	12%
Short films	11%
TV commercials	11%
Other	2%
None	11%

Note: n=1,827 ages 8-64 who have ever watched online video content;
*asked of respondents ages 18+
Source: Frank N. Magid Associates, "Magid Media Futures 2010: Online Video" sponsored by Metacafe, June 29, 2010

117004   www.eMarketer.com

Figure 1.1   Types of Online Video Views

Video, delivered via television, has been extensively proven to promote and improve brand recognition, conversions, and awareness for companies of all sizes. Its introduction and now full use delivered via the Internet is creating another layer of opportunities for you to reach your customers. I will use the term "conversions"often. Most marketers know what the term means, but just to be sure, I'll define it. The conversion rate is the ratio of visitors who convert casual content views or website visits into desired actions based on subtle or direct requests from marketers, advertisers, and content creators.

Video will soon be a necessary component in all successful marketing campaigns. It starts with you, the online marketer. You made it through the changes brought about by Google's search engine marketing, pay-per-click ad campaigns, and search engine optimization. You need to be a top performer in the use of innovative video content as a standard component of your marketing campaign to create a return on your marketing investment.

The use of video will continue to grow as the years pass. This is primarily because video can provide something that text-based content cannot: it allows you to see the person sharing the content; it builds trust in viewers; it develops a perception among viewers that they are dealing with a real person or company. Text-based content will always be available, but the demand for it is declining as more customers and prospective buyers view video content to gain the information they need for making purchasing decisions.

A report titled *Magid Media Futures 2010: Online Video* demonstrates that as of May 2010, at least 17 types of video content were available for viewers, including weather reports, standard-length films, sports events, music videos, commercials, and adult films. Only 11 percent of respondents had never viewed online content of any notable type.

Moore's Law

A book about Internet marketing would not be complete without mentioning Moore's Law. It holds that the number of transistors that can be inexpensively placed on an integrated circuit doubles every two years. This trend of inexpensively doubling the number of transistors on a circuit has continued for more than half a century. Because smooth play of online video requires specific hardware and software, including sufficient memory and processing power, viewing video would not be possible without the contribution of Moore's law to the history of computing hardware.

The impact of Moore's law is important to note because the capabilities of many digital devices that show video are strongly linked to the prediction it makes. These capabilities include processing speed, memory capacity, sensors, and pixels. The pixel count in digital cameras is critical because increased pixel capability allows for higher fidelity in the content captured in videos.

According to Fuor Digital's vice president of media technology and analytics, Josh Dreller, "The cost to deliver video is going down, broadband penetration is going up, broadband speeds are rising; cost of data storage is going down, cost to deliver video is going down, etc. All of these factors are contributing to online video's meteoric rise." He continues: "Even though there is still a question whether or not online video is eroding television audiences, no one is debating that online viewing is skyrocketing. The inevitable power of Moore's Law—the principle that technology gets more powerful and less expensive exponentially—is in play here."

Top 10 Online Video Properties Among US Internet Users, Ranked by Ads Viewed, Dec 2010

	Video ads (millions)	% reach	Ads per viewer
1. Hulu	1,227.9	8.6%	47.1
2. Tremor Media*	1,021.7	28.6%	11.8
3. Adap.tv*	681.5	19.0%	11.9
4. BrightRoll*	587.9	22.3%	8.7
5. Microsoft sites	423.0	13.7%	10.2
6. CBS Interactive	271.5	10.1%	8.9
7. AOL	231.9	11.5%	6.7
8. Undertone*	226.8	8.1%	9.2
9. Google sites	223.8	15.3%	4.8
10. TubeMogul*	174.1	14.2%	4.1
Total US internet audience	**5,910.6**	**49.1%**	**39.8**

Note: home, work and university locations; includes streaming video advertising only; excludes other types of monetization, such as overlays, branded players, matching banner ads, homepage ads, etc.; *video ad network
Source: comScore Video Metrix as cited in press release, Jan 21, 2011

124483   www.eMarketer.com

Figure 1.2   Top 10 Online Properties

The Nielsen Company reports that online video usage in the United States increased considerably in 2010. In the 12 months prior to this writing, time spent viewing video on personal desktops and laptops, at home and at work, increased by 45 percent. The number of unique online video viewers only increased by 3.1 percent from January 2011, but the level of activity increased as viewers streamed 28 percent more video and spent 45 percent more time watching it.

In January 2011, ComScore Video Metrix identified the top ten online video properties that U.S. Internet users rely on for their content. This report included the total number of ads delivered via video and the number of ads received on a per-viewer basis. Figure 1.2 provides a simple chart of this information. These figures represent grand opportunities for online marketers to place their advertising messages in front of viewers.

Bandwidth

Bandwidth refers to the rate at which information can be transmitted. The availability of bandwidth and its decreasing costs have facilitated the transition from text-based to video-based content. Today the cost is just a fraction of what it was when it first appeared in the technology world. Breakthroughs in video technology have made it much easier for video content to be shared with online viewers through methods referred to as streaming or progressive downloads. Whether you stream a video or serve it as a progressive download via a local server, the cloud, or broadband, know that each of these methods is making it easy and affordable for you to saturate your prospects with video content.

Cloud Computing

Ben Pring, senior analyst at Gartner Research, suggests that cloud computing has "become the phrase du jour." He echoes the perception many of his peers hold, that everyone seems to have a different definition of cloud computing. As with Web 2.0, it means something different to each industry professional. As a metaphor for the Internet, "the cloud" is a familiar cliché. When that same cliché is combined with the act of computing, its meaning becomes more abstract, ambiguous, and harder to pin down. I have found that some analysts and vendors define cloud computing as virtual servers available over the Internet. Others argue that cloud computing is any activity that occurs outside of your computer's immediate firewall, and this includes conventional outsourcing.

Regardless of the definition, know that the bottom line is that the cloud will bring many changes for your company in the world of marketing with video. More Web-based video tools will be available, and the cost to serve video on websites will decrease significantly. This will be followed by increased usage of video on individual websites. These additional tools and easily manageable cost structures will dispel budgetary arguments that may have impeded the use of video in the past. Now the use of video footage will become common on websites throughout the Web. The full value of video content on websites of various sizes and activity levels will be fully realized, and video will be embraced as the newest must-have in your marketing arsenal.

Video as a Marketing Tactic

The dramatic increase in the number of consumers watching online video provides enticing and encouraging information for marketers. The recent data collected provides important statistics on which to base marketing decisions. As you explore the opportunities that video marketing provides, even if you are new to this medium, just remember the basics of any good marketing campaign: make contact with the target market as often as you can in a decision-making environment. Each time you connect with a customer or prospective customer, you touch them. Touching customers and prospective customers can happen in many ways, including direct mail, e-mail, phone, and text message. Video should now be included in this list.

One of my own aha moments occurred when I realized that the difficulty of reaching customers online by the use of video was only a temporary problem. The technology did not always exist to deliver video content to viewers. Many devices were not even able to process video as recently as just a few years ago. This presented problems for marketers wanting to place video content on their website as a method of promoting their product or service. The technology was quickly evolving, yet many viewers continued to use dial-up connections. However, the technology for video delivery expanded, and so did my understanding that as video delivered via Internet grew, it would take hold of the Web and explode. It wasn't long before video began to overtake all other digital channels. It became a massive tool easily available to large and small advertisers with a product or service to sell. Marketers and advertisers with any size budget could now compete in ways they never could before.

It's disappointing that only a fraction of marketers today are using video technology to promote their brand or increase leads and generate sales-prompting actions taken by prospective customers. Every one of you could benefit from this technology, and soon you'll make it work for you to increase your leads and create sales conversions.

Video Trend Statistics

Hunter Walk, director of product management for YouTube, discussed the use of social media coverage and the related growth of YouTube in an interview immediately following the earthquake and tsunami that devastated Japan on Friday, March 11, 2011. Walk indicated that in less than one week following the initial disaster, more than 16,000 videos displaying footage of the crisis in Japan and containing an "earthquake" or "tsunami" tag were uploaded to YouTube. People consumed information about the event via online video. Thousands of videos were viewed online that showed the devastation of the tsunami. The hours of video footage, when added together, far surpassed the time spent by viewers watching the national news.

The numbers related to incorporating video into your marketing mix cannot to be ignored. Content delivered via video footage has shifted the consumer's perspective. Consumers are allowing video content to play a major part in their lives and happily give away their time to view the messages created:

• YouTube serves 1 billion videos to interested viewers every day. In 2011, the average person watched 182 online videos each month. Consumers have developed their consumption habits by watching videos via YouTube. This habit is critical information for online marketers: consumers want to receive your marketing information in a manner that is consistent with their consumption habits.

- Living Direct, an online retailer, determined that video content boosted conversions in addition to increasing consumers' website visit time by 9 percent (Internet Retailer, October 2010).
- Internet Retailer reported in April 2010 that visitors who view product videos are 85 percent more likely to buy than visitors who do not.
- ComScore reported in August 2010 that retail site visitors who view videos extend their website visit by an average of two minutes. These same visitors are 64 percent more likely to make a purchase than other website visitors.
- Frank Malsbenden, vice president and general manager of Vision Retailing Inc., the parent company of Shoeline.com, indicated that Shoeline.com experienced an increase in online sales conversions of 44 percent after implementing video footage to showcase their footwear. "With such positive results on our existing videos, the goal right now is to add video to as many of our products as possible," says Malsbenden.
- Zappos reported a 6 to 30 percent increase in product sales when providing consumers with video content, according to ReelSEO in December 2009.
- The L2 Specialty Retail Report indicated in September 2010 that retail sites containing video increase their conversion by 30 percent. These same sites also found that including video boosted their average sales ticket by 13 percent.

Case studies demonstrating the use of video provide further evidence that footage must accompany your marketing campaign for it to successfully increase conversions and provide a return on your investment. Three case studies have been included so you can understand how Napster, Tandberg, and Capitol Records got into action and used online video to promote their products. You can have similar success, and later chapters of this book will show you how.

Napster

Marketers at Napster, the top provider of unlimited on-demand streaming music, were singing the praises of using online video to convert visits into sales. The company decided to add video content to its website and noted that making just that one change

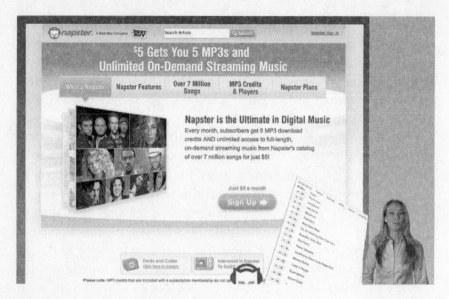

Figure 1.3 Napster's Online Video Spokesperson

generated an 18.5 percent increase in paid subscriptions and free trial sign-ups.

Napster's in-house marketing team conducted an A/B test. For the test, they created and used an online video spokesperson and included this spokesperson feature on their landing page versus the same landing page without the video spokesperson. Visitors came to their website from a combination of direct traffic, pay-per-click (PPC) traffic, and affiliate-driven traffic. All PPC ad offers matched the offer on the page. The landing page was the first page visitors saw. The only difference between the two testing versions was the addition of a 40-second "What You Get" video on version A.

"Welcome to Napster," the video began. "With Napster you get MP3 credits and on-demand music for one low price." Further highlights of the video's audio were included: "Use your MP3 credits to purchase any song or album you like. . . . The on-demand music gives you unlimited access to millions of songs."

Remarkably, the video converted more visitors even though it played anytime a visitor landed on the page, including repeat visitors. The video's relatively short 40-second length probably helped increase the conversions. There were controls in place that allowed visitors to pause or mute the video. This is an interesting test that you can try with your own company to monitor your results and determine whether your campaign needs adjusting. This test would work especially well for subscription sites. Keep in mind that Napster is a subscription service, and like other Internet sites that provide ongoing opportunities to subscribe and pay for products or services, your own results will depend on your subscribers and your product, service, and promotion.

Tandberg

Tandberg manufactures small and large video conferencing systems. They were acquired by Cisco in 2010. At that time, the product portfolio of Cisco video conferencing solutions and the Tandberg systems were combined into a single portfolio. The Tandberg product names have since changed, and there are still product overlaps in their portfolio, but some are still offered under the Tandberg brand name. When the company was direct marketing under the Tandberg name, their goal was to get website visitors who were interested in video conferencing equipment to fill out a sales lead form.

The promotion was a new video for their voice-over-internet protocol (VoIP) high-resolution video in one easy-to-use device. The product's visual capabilities were highlighted when a video was included on the screen of the phone. A video spokesperson appeared to be speaking to the viewer via the VoIP and repeating the keyword from Google that Tandberg was buying. For all leads received, a company sales person would provide further information and answer their questions about products. Tandberg's sales lead form is a short message received via their website that contains a prospective customer's contact information. The lead is routed to the sales team for action. Tandberg received a boost in their conversion rate of 3.5 to 7 percent when they structured their online video to repeat the keyword on which they were advertising.

For example, if traffic came from their Google pay-per-click ad for keyword "VoIP," the video greeted visitors by confirming that the website knew they were "looking for information on voice over IP." If visitors were directed from the keyword "Tandberg," the video assured them that they were on the Tandberg direct site and not a reseller's site. The formula of repeating the keyword from Google search clicks made a significant impact in their conversion rates. Highlights of the video spokesperson's welcome to visitors included, "Are you looking for information on voice over IP? Well, welcome to Tandberg. We are reinventing the desk phone—it's voice, it's video, and Tandberg is making it easy." The consumer who clicked was assured by the video that they were in the right place, and this allowed Tandberg to finish their selling proposition.

Unlike Napster, Tandberg did not conduct a straight A/B test. Because Tandberg was tracking their website visitors and conversions in other ways, the increase in conversions became significant. In fact, their result was much better than anything they had seen on other similar pages where they asked a customer to fill out a sales lead form in exchange for more information.

Capitol Records

Fifty-two percent of users watched a two-minute video from start to finish, and Capitol Records' promotional unit noted a 14 percent click-through rate during this process. The record company, as part of their promotion of country music singer Trace Adkins, created

Figure 1.4 Capitol Records—Trace Adkins Promotion

25 unique Trace Adkins videos. Each unique video aired on a different country music radio station across the United States. The promotional videos were customized with the singer mentioning the radio station's call letters for each station at which the videos would be aired. "Welcome to 92.5 XTU," Adkins greeted listeners and website visitors. "Click me to buy my new album." The overall goal of the video was to get radio station listeners and website visitors to visit a specific promotion page, provide an e-mail address, and take a chance at winning a prize.

The most important aspect of this campaign is that the viewers watched the video to the very last frame—52 percent of viewers watched the full two-minute video. The video's success was an important contribution to the campaign. I've never seen such a great result without the implementation of video footage.

Video Is Everywhere

In the twenty-first century, the world around us is being captured on video by both the professional media and ordinary citizens. These videos are capturing the details of life every moment of every day. Anything that can be celebrated is captured; anything that is noteworthy is captured. Even those fleeting glimpses into the general activities of everyday life that are considered to be of no consequence are captured and added to the circulation of data living above the world in that space called the Internet.

Taking your product or service beyond general text and graphics requires video. Consumers expect more from brands and brand messages today. They expect brands to make it easy for the product or service to communicate a value proposition. What they are looking for is a conversation, and video creates the feel of conversation for customers and potential customers. Many factors need to be taken into consideration in moving your company to video. I'll show you the elements that will make your video work on a large or small scale. You'll have the capability, with video, to increase your company's conversions, and it won't matter if you're a small business person or a multinational marketer.

Video Can Build Trust

Video is exciting, informative, and profitable for many businesses. Video can put an authentic face on your company, product, or service. Footage that you present to your viewers will catch their eye. The movement, color, sound, and action make it nearly impossible for viewers to resist looking. It is also a simple way to convey multiple emotions to viewers with few or no words. Nearly everyone watches video content. Using video will allow you to personalize your brand, your product, and your service.

Using footage is a cool tactic to implement when you want to focus on something promotional or educational. Putting video to work for you can decrease the time it takes for prospective customers to feel that they trust you long before they actually talk with you or others at your company.

There are many solutions available and probably already included in your marketing plan. Video is a solution that requires creative discipline and technical knowledge to produce. You probably relied confidently upon only text-based media and graphics for all marketing efforts you made to communicate your story—until the Internet was born.

You may have a perception that incorporating video into your marketing plan and using it as a tool to reach and connect with your customers is an unfamiliar, costly black hole. In fact, it can be, and sound guidance is available to help you make the right decisions and invest only what is necessary to get your video footage produced and making you money.

Unfortunately, video has another reputation to overcome. For some there is a perception that video is easy to produce and can be prepared even by a teenager in a garage or dorm room. Would that be appropriate for your brand or conversion efforts? Is that the perception you want customers to have of your product or service?

Blendtec's series of videos have done very well with smaller budgets and have also received 150,000 views on their YouTube channel for their commercial-grade footage. Your company can compete better for the attention of your audiences by using similar content and getting it in front of your customers.

But they must see it. Getting video through to customers and prospective customers is no longer a challenge, with delivery systems easily available to serve the footage for you. In fact, serving the video over the Web and mobile media was once more complicated than producing the content. There are a number of online video platforms (OVPs) developed exclusively to help businesses and online marketers serve video and remove the headaches associated with it. Look for the discussion in chapter 6 about delivery options for your newly produced video content.

The other side of the perception that video is a black hole are the marketers who are looking for a well-produced video that requires sophisticated equipment, a movie studio with trained technicians, and professional cast members. When thinking about producing video footage for your online marketing program, you may mistakenly use the production of a television commercial as your benchmark for what is involved. But producing a television commercial is much more complicated and labor intensive than a common Web video. Don't let this preconceived notion make you nervous.

The reality is that both options are available. There is also a sizable market for inexpensive, quality video products and services that occupies the area between the teen producer and the professional footage director. Popular culture only increases the number of videos available on the Internet, and it adds to the noise and competitive clutter you can expect when promoting your product or service online. There is good news: you will prevail when you understand that video must now be included in your customer communication efforts.

Conversions and Branding

Conversions are frequently referred to in the world of marketing via the Internet. Conversions are calculated as the number of visitors visiting your website who make a particular action because of that visit. Conversions are measured as a ratio of the desired actions that your company wants website visitors to make.

Branding is the implicit perception that your video viewers will have of your company. Your website visitors, customers, and prospects that you continue to check in with regularly all have a perception of your company. Their perception involves what they think your company does, your expertise, and the potential results you can create for them when they hire your company.

Trust me when I say that your conversions can increase by adding video to your campaigns. Returns on investment (ROIs) will be discussed at length in chapter 5. Remember, step by step I'll walk you through the information you need to know to be a leader in your field. Just be patient because it all ties together.

In 2004, technology skyrocketed, and the video production industry saw a variety of versions of video technology. The growth of graphics-based content delivered via video was evident in rich media, pre-roll video, YouTube, and G4 mobile—for starters. Each of these technologies made a contribution to brand awareness in addition to increased sales conversions and sales leads. Leads could be transformed from product awareness into buyers willing to take out their credit cards or open their wallets to make a purchase. This willingness can be described as the desired action you want your website visitors to take. Video can increase your conversions. Use it to your advantage.

Online Video Increases Conversions

The Interactive Advertising Bureau determined that it took 38 years for radio to reach 50,000,000 users, 13 years for television, 10 years for cable, less than 5 years for Internet, and less than 2 years for online video. Consumers from all walks of life watch more online video now than ever before. Heavy online video users continue to increase their online video consumption while at the same time decreasing their offline television consumption. Despite these trends, online video advertising costs remain just a fraction of that spent overall on all advertising.

ComScore determined that more and more Americans are watching online video. They pegged the average at 19.5 hours per viewer in just the month of September 2011. They put the number of Americans who enjoyed video online for some purpose within that same month at 182 million.

Sales leads and sales conversions escalate when you combine visuals, text, and audio together. Viewers can absorb much more information in a shorter period of time when all methods are served concurrently. Learning studies have demonstrated that content is up to three times more likely to be retained when it is delivered with video.

You can take your website to the next level by including video content for your consumers. Businesses tend to explain products or services on a Web page in a text format. This is a flat, one-dimensional experience for visitors. When using video, you bring your company's story to life and ensure that your viewer has a better

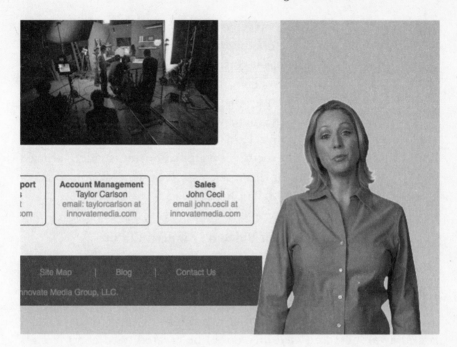

Figure 1.5 Video Spokesperson Example

US Online Video Viewers, 2009-2015							
	2009	**2010**	**2011**	**2012**	**2013**	**2014**	**2015**
Online video viewers (millions)	130.8	145.6	158.1	169.3	178.7	187.6	195.5
—% change	13.1%	11.3%	8.6%	7.1%	5.6%	5.0%	4.2%
—% of population	42.6%	46.9%	50.5%	53.5%	56.0%	58.2%	60.1%
—% of internet users	60.5%	65.0%	68.2%	70.8%	72.9%	74.7%	76.0%

Note: CAGR (2009-2015)=6.9%; internet users who download or stream video online via any device at least once per month
Source: eMarketer, Feb 2011

124217   www.eMarketer.com

Figure 1.6 US Online Video Viewers

understanding of your message as they make it through interview clips, product demos, and whiteboard walkthroughs.

You may even decide to include a video spokesperson in your footage. A spokesperson delivering your company's message via video units can be the most personal of all online video examples. Including a spokesperson to deliver a message in your video content allows you to literally walk out of the computer screen to tell your story to your viewer. This is as personal as it gets. Some video producers use actors rather than a video spokesperson. The actors can also help build a sense of personal trust in a way that television commercials cannot.

With the explosion of inexpensive bandwidth, you can now offer video and not worry about load times. In fact, Forbes Insights found that 75 percent of executives watched business videos at least weekly, with 65 percent of those taking a follow-up action to learn more, call a vendor, or make a purchase.

The Influence of Video on Modern Culture

Online video is not really that different. Video been used since the 1950s on television. A whole medium was developed around video. If we talk specifically about the ad community, television commercials were effective in promoting a product or service to viewers. Brand awareness and visibility could be created with commercials placed throughout viewers' content. The three-dimensional nature of video correlated well with the television medium for prompting viewers to take an action or buy a product. Now, though, viewers are making a shift from text-based matter to video-based content received via the Internet.

"Video is pushing the boundaries of what's possible in online advertising, and it's growing at a rate of 40 percent year-over-year," says Dave Otten. "Any marketer worth their salt knows they have to buy video if they aren't already." Everything that worked in the offline setting must now be available for online viewing. But video is different from other media available for capturing and displaying your message to viewers, such as graphics, photos, or icons.

Marshall McLuhan used the phrase "the medium is the message" as a means of conveying how the distribution of a message can often be more important than the content of the message itself. The strong social and cultural impact that video has had on society is predicated upon its ability to reach a massive audience with a well-constructed and influential message.

McLuhan was the first person to popularize the concept of a global village and to consider its social effects. His insights were revolutionary at the time, and they fundamentally changed how marketers worldwide think about media, technology, and communications. McLuhan chose the insightful phrase "global village" to highlight his observation that an electronic nervous system (the media) was rapidly integrating the planet, such that events in one part of the world could be experienced in other places in real time, which is what the human experience is like for those who live in small villages.

Television broadcasting has had a lot of control over the content that society watches, and over when society watches it. This is a distinguishing feature of traditional media, and Internet video has challenged this feature by altering the participation habits of the viewing public. The Internet has created space for more diverse political opinions, more varied social and cultural viewpoints, and a heightened level of consumer participation. There have been suggestions that allowing consumers to produce information through the Internet will lead to an overload of information.

The online video medium available today is the heartbeat of our world's electronic nervous system. It requires that marketers understand the revolutionary and evolutionary quality of it, in addition to how this new platform combines the traits of television with those of the Internet.

Video Cannot Be Ignored

Today, nearly every video project produced by Innovate Media prompts a satisfied online marketer to refer their colleagues to us. When we first opened our doors for business in 2002, we produced about 20 videos a year. In 2012, we will produce well over 600. Part of this estimate includes content produced using the video spokesperson feature. Think of these as little clips rather than full-fledged videos.

Despite its ability to significantly impact customers' purchase life cycle, increase brand awareness, and drive the number of visitors to businesses' websites, online video advertising largely remains an untapped opportunity. Hollywood entertainment moguls have voraciously cracked the code on the use of effective online video advertising better than any other industry. Each movie made today has a specifically produced two-minute trailer. This trailer runs in a pre-roll position on the movie's video website in addition to the 30-second spot that television viewers see. This combination is a winner. Viewers can go to the website after they have seen the commercial. They can immediately determine if the film appeals to them, and they may purchase tickets to view the film at a theater near them.

All of the discussion and information in this chapter is so you can see that this transition to video is occurring, and it's moving quickly. Your company can move with it or let it pass them by. To make the most of your marketing dollars, it is imperative that incorporating video content into your current marketing plan becomes a priority.

In this chapter, you learned the following:

☑ Video has been proven to increase conversions;
☑ Consumer trends in video consumption are transitioning to the online marketer;
☑ What customers will remember about your video message.

Now you can understand that video must be integrated into your customers' lives in many ways, right now, today. As you read, you'll learn about the video styles available, and you'll see that they may easily be used in your purchase funnel. Keep in mind that it doesn't all have to happen today, at this moment. Just go one step at a time. Stick with me. I'll also share with you my eight golden rules of video . . . one step at a time.

CHAPTER 2

Video in the Media Mix:
Where It's Been and Where It's Going

I f you look at the impact video has on our daily lives, it's easy to see that your customers live a life very similar to yours, and you live a life similar to mine. Video influences each of us on a daily basis. Your customers go about their daily lives enjoying video throughout the day, receiving news, surfing the Internet, checking out weather reports, looking up recipes, and so much more. Consumers hear about your product and they visit your website to find out more information. At that point they become a prime target to convert to a customer. However, instead of reaching them with video, as they now experience content in all other aspects of their lives, you greet them with text and graphics. The process by which you are marketing to your customers today probably does not include video. Television is very different from video, and you'll need to step back from your perceptions about television so that you can fully embrace video, get your footage created for online viewing, and smile about the increase video is making in your sales.

A Day in a Life—Yours, Mine, and Your Customers'

We see video and feel the difference video makes in all aspects of our lives. When I wake up in the morning, I am involved in video in several ways. Online I check the highlights from last night's sports events. I see the video content replaying right before my eyes, the shots that won the game that I was too busy to attend. Watching

ESPN and other sports videos is how I get my information now. No more reading articles, website content, or lengthy text materials. I'm ready for action the minute my Internet browser finishes loading. The Lakers play before my eyes in their gold and purple uniforms. The jump shots to score, the blocks, and the traveling offenses called by the referee move before me, and I experience their basketball game as if I were in the front row of the court.

As we travel to the neighborhood school for drop-off each morning, my children are involved with video, too. My daughter watches anything that Disney produces, and my son is busy with content about trains. They always want video. Images. Captured. Things they will remember seeing. At the office, an increasing percentage of my communication is now conducted through Skype video. Images. Visual connection. More stuff to remember. I constantly talk to people through the Web. We are online together. It's all video. And we haven't even begun to talk about the video cameras that record our every move at offices, parking lots, street corners, banks, shopping centers, restaurants, or public transportation. Video is touching our lives where we expect it and where we don't expect it. It's the same for your customers. Video content is critical to their decision to buy from you. That's life. Text has shifted to video content that is available around the clock via the Internet.

Television? It's rare in my life that I watch anything on the set that was once so popular in our home. Newspapers sit untouched in my office lobby. Actually, they're there for customers waiting to talk about the final cuts of their video footage. I don't read them. I love media. I want the glitz, color, and action delivered right to me. Write this down: your customers want the glitz, color, and action of online video content delivered right to them!

Personally, I believe that the impact of video on my life is positive. It's a good thing. Yes, I'm a lot closer to this technology than most people are since I wrapped my career around video production and delivery. I analyze content every day. Nevertheless, from my view, it's a quality-of-life issue. The advancement of technology is influencing and improving my life and the lives of those I love. Video may be on the list of great inventions like the washing machine, clothes dryer, dishwasher, and microwave oven. The human connection involved in video and the trust it can create for companies has the ability to improve our lives. When we let it influence our actions and our relationships, they will be better. I have a greater connection with my customers when I use Skype. Your customers will have better relationships when you serve them video content for their online purchasing decisions.

My customers, family members, and I download movies to view via iPad. The whole mobile world is changing, and it is becoming a world filled with online video content. Recently, I've noticed how much time I spend watching YouTube videos, and that time has increased from past months. Much but not all of my entertainment content comes from YouTube. A lot of it is short clips and video snaps rather than long-form programming. Watching *Saturday Night Live* while relaxing at home has been replaced with online video clips of the show that are available via the Web. Video has changed my life. It has changed your customers' lives, and it will change your life—if it hasn't already.

Television versus Video

YuMe found that 49 percent of people are watching videos daily for an average total of seven hours per week per person. YuMe is a video ad company that conducted a survey in 2011 of online video watchers. These survey results further confirm the necessity of including video as a primary marketing tool.

Seven hours is roughly equal to 3.5 full-length movie films back to back. Seven hours is nearly a full workday. Leaving from Los Angeles, California, you would get about halfway to the island of Fiji in seven hours. Seven hours is a lot when you realize that 70 percent of the content being viewed is considered short-form

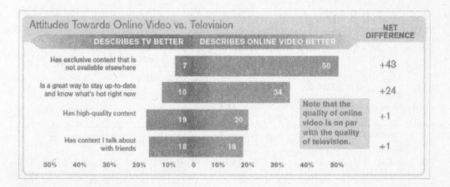

Figure 2.1 Attitudes Graph

video. Videos in this category are typically less than five minutes long. Four hundred twenty minutes of short-form video content could be more than 84 videos per person per week. Television still reigns as the top choice for long-form content. The tide is shifting, though, and more video content was enthusiastically consumed somewhere on the Web while you read these words.

The majority of people surveyed by YuMe indicated their appreciation of the flexibility that video provides. Content can be consumed, and is consumed, at any hour of any day, whenever the consumer desires. This is indeed a major change over the use of television. Online viewers described video as having content that is not readily available in other places, allowing them to stay current on specific topics or news items. The quality of video and television were ranked similarly. Viewers admitted their easy willingness to talk about online video content with their friends in a manner like that for television.

Keep reading and you'll learn the following:

- ☑ How text has shifted to video, as have your customer's consumption habits;
- ☑ How video was developed and why you need to use it;
- ☑ How the lives of your customers are focused around video;
- ☑ How the marketing purchase funnel applies to the video world.

Text has shifted to video. Do you have a pen and paper? Write this down: *Text has shifted to video.* Yes, I did repeat myself, and with good reason. If you're not using video, well, your customers aren't customers, are they? They probably just left your website to click on your competitor's site to watch a video about the product they want to purchase. You could have made that sale. Too bad video content wasn't included on your site.

Michael Zimbalist describes the shift from text to video this way: "We are media omnivores. We like choice and variety." Zimbalist is the vice president of research and development operations for the *New York Times*. In this position, Zimbalist has been sitting in the front row of life's theater and has seen the change firsthand. Interestingly, he suggests that "the media marketplace today resembles what ecologists might call an evolutionary stable state . . . in an ecosystem of many different analog and digital media devices, co-existing in harmony." If in fact Zimbalist is right, then this contributes to the high level of viewer abandonment many websites experience in the final phases of the online sales process. This abandonment often occurs because the site consists of words and photos, with little or no information available via attractive video content.

If you are new to the industry, "abandonment" is a term used by online marketers that addresses the issue of visitors leaving a website without taking any action. Desired actions are typically buying a product, picking up the phone to call, or filling out a lead form to request more information. In the perspective of marketers, leaving without taking an action is not a desirable result. Many things can lead to abandonment. It doesn't matter if your website is expensive or was done on the cheap; either may be affected.

When we talk about delivery of your video content in chapter 6, you will learn that it is possible to determine if a viewer watches your online content to the last frame. You can also identify points where they drop from viewing. When you can get your viewers to watch your video to the very last frame, they are more likely to buy, and that's what you want—a conversion. Why customers leave a video and what you can do to create videos that viewers will watch to completion are critical points to track.

We don't want your marketing funds spent investing in Gen 1.0 digital media experiences where text is used to market to your customers. That's not what you want. Remember, text and still graphics are shifting to video content. Video is sophisticated and increasingly easy to use. Moving pictures delivered via video are necessary for your new strategy. For you to truly understand how to use video effectively as a key tool in your overall marketing campaigns and customer strategies, it is important that you understand how video developed.

The Birth of Video

Famous actor and singer Bing Crosby has the distinction of presenting to the world the first demonstration of a videotaped recording. A division of his production company pitched it to Los Angeles viewers on November 11, 1951. They saw for the first time what looked like worn-out motion picture images. The video was essentially produced and recorded on magnetic tape. It was made of a thin magnetic coating on a long, narrow strip of plastic. This occurred before the birth of digital media. Video constantly evolved, getting better with each step. Now consumers cannot live without it.

Have you met Max? Max Headroom was the first cyberpunk series to run in the United States. The series ran on one of the main broadcast networks during prime time. He was a fictitious British artificial intelligence figure. Max was known for his wit and his stuttering, distorted, electronically sampled voice. Max Headroom was featured in a music video program, a feature film, a dramatic television series, television commercials, and the song "Paranoimia" by the British pop act Art of Noise. His name was derived from the phrase "maximum headroom."

The Max Headroom Show was later developed into the British television movie *Max Headroom: 20 Minutes into the Future*. This in turn evolved into the pilot for a series which ran from 1987 to 1988. The first episode was presented to American audiences in an extended edition on Cinemax in 1986. Though it was officially set up for two seasons, only 14 episodes were created, and of those only 13 were aired.

Max Headroom was a landmark in the development of video entertainment. His creators demonstrated that adults could be readily entertained by a phantom character who only lived in the space of technology. He was fully a figment of our imaginations. The series also had an impact on how viewers received information because the trend in video editing shifted to provide viewers with "a sequence of rapidly changing images." This was done to increase the thrill and excitement a viewer would experience while viewing. This type of rapid-fire imagery was demonstrated in music videos and promotional messages delivered on movie television channels and in mainstream television commercials during the late 1980s and early 1990s.

The CBS television network reported in 2004 that a *blipvert effect* occurs when moving through advertising commercials in fast-forward mode, and this blipvert effect can increase viewers' recall of the advertiser's message. General Electric started a series of *One Second Theater* commercials during which many frames of information were compressed into the single second of a 30-second commercial. These were both demonstrations of rapid-fire imagery that evolved after Max Headroom made his appearance in households across the United States.

Professor Byron Reeves, at Stanford University's Center for the Study of Language and Information, conducted a study that supports the use of a video spokesperson in video content. The study found that "characters can express social roles, emotions, and organized personalities that match learning goals, company brands, and transaction needs. Characters can increase the trust that users place in online experiences, in part because they make online experiences easier." Research on interactive characters suggests "substantial opportunities for them to enhance online experiences." Reeves determined that "automated characters take advantage of social responses that are natural reactions to interactive media. They can be perceived as realistic and well-liked social partners in conversations that simulate real-world interactions."

Max Headroom, perhaps the first video spokesperson, first demonstrated this growing trend in the use of video. Technological advancements now available have increased the quality of production and the delivery of content to viewers. A spokesperson delivered with video content, whether named Max or not, has proven to be very effective in generating trust among viewers who relate to video characters rather than text and static images. Thank you, Max.

Images Forever Engrained in Our Memory

Images tend to become engrained in our memories forever. It doesn't matter whether these memories are pleasant, sad, horrific, or of disastrous occasions. They are forever imprinted in our minds, and we can recall them at will. Many such memories recur to us regularly, while others are remembered each time an anniversary rolls around or when the news media points their microphone toward it.

If you're married, one of your memories is your wedding day. You played a part in the event when it occurred; you looked at the pictures after the photographer sent the proofs or your friends gave you copies of shots they captured. Memories. Images. Forever. Weddings are a happy experience, a time when we are surrounded by those who love us and whom we love, marking this occasion together. In your memory, you've got stored many of these occasions. There may be a few weddings, births, or promotions, your child's first steps or first words, bar mitzvahs, grand openings, or other times that fill you with delight. It's just important to remember that they are there. Images in your mind.

National or world events also create images forever in our minds. Several pivotal events include the Los Angeles riots brought about by the beating of Rodney King, the assassination of President John F. Kennedy, the bombing of the World Trade Center, and the explosion of the *Challenger* space shuttle on January 28, 1986.

A top moment in the history of user-generated video content occurred in 1996 when Rodney King was videotaped as he received a beating by Los Angeles police officers. The footage was captured by a witness to the violence. Many Americans remember this event and the images they witnessed of the published video footage.

At the time it occurred, this type of recording was unheard of. Most media clips were taped by the television networks themselves. None had been taped by or were available from ordinary citizens using their personal video cameras. Today it's a common occurrence to view video clips of special unscripted events recorded by people who post them on YouTube or another website with file-sharing capability. These unscripted events captured by ordinary people in real-world situations may be of someone breaking the law, or silly pet tricks, and everything in between.

Looking back more than a century ago, Dr. Zapruder filmed footage on his home camera while standing in the crowd of people watching John F. Kennedy's presidential limousine pass by. *Life* magazine and its owner, *Time*, subsequently purchased the footage from Zapruder and preserved it for more than 40 years. There were thoughts that the American public was not ready to view footage depicting such a horrific event. Finally it was released for public viewing. Dick Gregory and Robert Groden, assassination researchers, presented the first showing of the Zapruder home footage on ABC's late-night show, *Good Night America*, on March 6, 1975. The outrage experienced by the viewing public led to the Hart-Schweiker investigation, an investigation by the House Select Committee on Assassination, and impacted the Church Committee Investigation on Intelligence Activities.

The space shuttle *Challenger* exploded 73 seconds into its voyage on January 28, 1986. Seven crew members died immediately as the spacecraft disintegrated over the Atlantic Ocean. This event was taped by network television stations present at the launch. The footage was shown hundreds of times after the event on various television programs. This moment was captured forever, and is forever in our minds.

Videotaped images of the planes that crashed into the World Trade Center and the Pentagon on September 11, 2001, were recorded by ordinary citizens. User-generated content accidentally captured the surprising images of the first building. Footage of the second tower was captured by networks on location who were present to film the devastation that occurred after the first tower was hit. Images forever in our minds. User-generated and professional content.

Video has changed television news forever. There was a time when news crews would travel around town to capture news as it was happening. That's no longer the case. News channels today often receive clips of user-generated content. These clips are sent to them by myriad sources, and the news organizations may use it as is, modify it, or expand it to fit the spot available and the circumstances it depicts. The news networks telecast it and add context to the media captured by a local citizen. Other examples of user-generated content telecast by news networks include hurricane and tornado footage provided by storm chasers.

Television influenced Americans during the Kennedy/Nixon presidential campaign debates. These debates were a prime example of television's ability to exert influence over viewers to meet a particular outcome or achieve a desired result. Newsmakers today use television to reach people throughout the world. Media is also penetrating closed and semi-closed cultures and has varying degrees of influence on North Korean society and the regime changes occurring in the Middle East.

The music industry exploded with audio and video footage. This footage led to the exposure of artists and their capabilities to viewers worldwide. These artists in turn sometimes used media to promote their work, whether music, audio, or video, to a broader audience. Live television spotlighted the Beatles as the greatest band in the world.

Ted Turner, WTBS television CEO, launched his cable television network and pleasantly surprised media content makers with the profit potential of providing viewers with vertical topics.

Turner found that presenting topics to viewers 24 hours a day with one programming theme could also create an explosion in specific product and service marketing. He proved that targeting specific audiences with extremely tailored messages delivered through video content could impact profits in a positive way. He provided images and influenced viewers. And you will too. You get where I'm going with this, right? It's important that you're on board and fully understand that you need to incorporate video every time you make contact with your customers.

Broadband evolved to create a platform for highly produced video content in popular culture. This evolution also serves business-to-business interactions with industrial or commercial content for product sales and services in every industry. The implementation of broadband has allowed companies to flood you with images.

These are all events that actually occurred. They were captured on video, and they will live throughout history. I'll bet that the people daring to press the "record" buttons to preserve these clips had no idea that these images would be critical to the world's evolution from text to video.

Google-Delivered Video Can Be Quickly Searched and Streamed

Business operations and methods have changed under Google's influence. Google itself has changed the way business is conducted because the executives watching where their company must step next have seen that search results are shifting to include video-related content in addition to text-based websites. My son and I thank you, Google, for helping with our recent project. Box, parts, boy anxious to ride his new bicycle, father fumbling with wrenches and tools to get the parts into the right places…After some exasperation, I checked online for help assembling this new Schwinn bike. I used Google to find a video of a bike similar to the one I had purchased for my son, and the guy in the video walked me through the installation and testing of the bike that now happily races up and down our street with a smiling boy peddling his fastest. Watching the video was better than reading an assembly manual.

The video that Google helped me find made the process of assembling my son's bike very easy. I searched, I found a video. My life was easier, and the project was completed faster because of online video content. Search engines are also changing. Search results are shifting from text to video content also. When you search for something, you will get listings for video content, not just text. This trend will only grow as more video content is placed online. Video search engine optimization (SEO) will be the next frontier for search capabilities, and I'll talk about that in chapter 8. Google sees this, and we can see adjustments being made to address this sector of the market. During a search with video SEO, you'll begin to see what is essentially a preview of what a video will show you before you click through to the site to view it. Cool, right? And another reason to make sure you provide video content online for your customers.

The Purchase Funnel—In a Non-Video World

Similar to the traditional marketing-based purchase funnel, the video purchase funnel describes the stages consumers go through when making a decision to buy something due to the influence a video has had on them. Notwithstanding spontaneous purchases

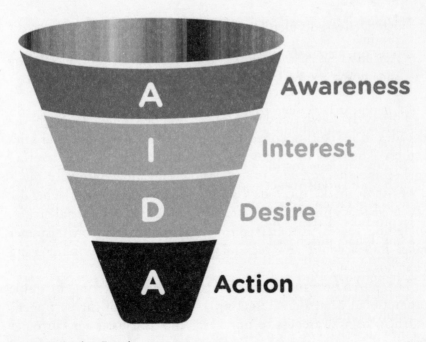

Figure 2.2 Purchase Funnel

made via online checkout counters or in brick-and-mortar establishments, consumers make conscious and unconscious decisions during each stage of the buying process. Highlights of these stages will help you see the importance of the purchase funnel. The stages of the buying process described by the purchase funnel are the shift from awareness to interest, desire, evaluation, and action.

A purchase funnel describes the journey your customer makes toward the purchase of your product or service. American advertising advocate Elmo Lewis wrote and spoke prolifically about the potential of advertising to educate the public. Lewis developed a model that mapped a fictitious customer's journey from the moment a brand or product attracted his or her attention to the point that the customer took action or made a purchase. The theory Lewis developed is the AIDA model. AIDA, in this case, is an acronym for awareness, interest, desire, and action. The stages of the process Lewis described are listed here for easy review:

- Awareness—the customer is aware that a product or service exists.
- Interest—the customer actively expresses interest in a product or service.
- Desire—the customer aspires to a particular brand or product.
- Action—the customer takes the next step toward purchasing the chosen product.

This early Lewis model has been handed down through the decades to marketing consultants, marketing educators, and sales leaders. The modern version has evolved in the world of marketing to become the *purchase funnel*. Many consumer purchase models exist in marketing today, and all are different. It is generally accepted that this modern purchase funnel has additional stages, including these: customer considers repurchase intent, customer takes into account new technologies, and customer's purchasing behavior changes.

The purchase funnel concept is used in marketing to guide promotional campaigns targeting various stages of the customer's journey from awareness to purchase, and as a basis for customer relationship management (CRM) programs.

The Video Purchase Funnel—In a Video World

One of the changes in technology that has caused a huge change in consumer purchase behavior is video. The purchase funnel without video has been modified to reflect and incorporate the use of online video content. I'll refer to it as the *video purchase funnel* because it is different from prior funnel models and allows for repurchase intent, new technologies, and changes in consumer purchasing behavior. Incorporating video offers more consumer control and therefore adds "unique to the Web" actions that are not found in the traditional funnel model. Video, in the video purchase funnel, changes every aspect of the AIDA concept:

- Awareness—the customer sees a video of a product on the product's site.
- Interest—the customer sends the video or a video e-mail to someone else and demonstrates an interest in the product.
- Desire—the customer feels a connection to the brand due to perceived pre-approval of the video that has been viewed and shared.
- Action—the customer clicks through to the product purchase page to further view product-related videos during the check-out process.

The AIDA purchase funnel is a primary reason for the growth of video, for example, in the fashion and publishing industries. This explains the many media print vehicles, from magazines to direct-marketing catalogs, available for customers to use in making their buying decisions. When consumers go to a website and see text, generally they are seeing the same thing they can find in magazines and catalogs. With print or text media, there is no experience or engagement. Video produced for fashion creates an up-close and personal experience that has always been a primary element in boosting sales as well as for the fashion industry itself. Leaders in fashion design rely on attribution. Service providers and product promoters for the fashion industry know this. They rely on it and use it to their advantage. Attribution is a process used to monitor the stages of media influence and touch points that consumers leverage during their process of making a purchase. You want to be a smart marketer who ensures that the last thing a consumer views before making a purchase is your online video content. Do it—video works!

You've learned much in this chapter including the following:

- ☑ Text has shifted to video, and so have your customers' consumption habits;
- ☑ How video was developed and why you need to use it;
- ☑ How your customers' daily lives are centered around video and how your text-based marketing must shift to include video;
- ☑ The marketing purchase funnel—with video added—applies to your customers.

Now you can see the importance of video and its effect on your marketing efforts. The global influence of this medium affects every living person. The use of text for your marketing messages has shifted to the use of online video. This shift has evolved over time, and you've been a part of it even if you don't know it. Many events captured throughout the world are stored in your memory as video footage, little snips, shots, and pictures. Is there a line of text under that memory that indicates what it is? Probably not. You inherently understand just from looking at the content your mind has produced or recalled for you. Your customers will do the same with your brand, your product, or your service after you provide them with online video content to make those first marks on their memory.

CHAPTER 3

Participate in the Video Revolution

You learned about the purchase funnel in chapter 2 and how the traditional purchase funnel must now be considered a video purchase funnel. Video has been added to the traditional purchase funnel because methods for creating online visibility with brand advertising and marketing are shifting to video. That means less text.

There are two camps in the marketing world, brand marketing and conversion marketing. When you market for conversions, all you care about is a sale, the amount you spend on advertising, how many customers you convert, and your conversion rate. Not much matters if the conversions are not present. The primary focus of this book is assisting you with increasing conversions for your brand. You are actively marketing your product or service, and you want more sales. You care about sales, sales, sales.

Brand advertising is more of a broad-stroke approach to marketing. A lot of money is spent to create a brand that ultimately leads to sales—for example, a Budweiser commercial that has nothing to do with beer because it's just a comedy sketch craftily created to entertain and promote the brand. More people buy more beer if the beer company does a good job with their branding. It works. Traditionally, most brand marketing has been accomplished through television spots. Video has been an incredible vehicle for companies to brand their products on television via commercials, infomercials, or long-form videos.

On the other side of the coin, conversion marketers have transitioned to the Web because that medium is better suited for conversions and sales leads. Remember, all of this is in a pre-video world. And keep in mind that some brand marketing is performed online, and some conversion marketing is done via television.

Video and the principles discussed in the following chapters will provide more opportunity for brand marketers online. Since video is currently being used on television to brand so many products, online video will eventually allow marketers to brand their products on the Internet. It may be that brand marketers know television like the back of their hand but are stuck in an offline world because they haven't realized the opportunities available for brand marketing via online video. Television is an important distribution vehicle for brand marketers. It allows them to brand their products to wide audiences, and they don't really need an online presence. Now that video can be used online, I expect that increasing numbers of brand marketers will use the Web to their advantage and build their brand with a concurrent online presence. It's happening now, though not with any great speed.

Popular brand advertising on the Web is not as prevalent as it could be. There is much debate as to the reason. One thing is clear: when the creative community and their brand advertisers recognize that text is losing steam for marketing to their customers, their habits will shift and they will enthusiastically jump in with both feet and get their video campaigns in front of their customers' eyes.

As you read this chapter, remember the principles of video: it's a sequence of images, and those images have an inherent ability to engage online viewers to promote your product or service. Video lengths vary, and industry standards are typically two, five, and ten minutes. Twenty minutes of video can serve particular purposes for some organizations and their viewers. But it's important to evaluate your video needs to determine if that length or if several short spots will work equally well while giving your viewers the content you need them to see. You need to know what video content style will be most effective for your customers. You can use more than one style, or use them all. Without a starting place, though, it will be difficult for you to visualize where to begin and what content you must use to connect with your customers.

The fact that technology is transitioning from text to video means that you now have greater opportunities to use the medium presented by video for increased conversions and stronger identification of your brand. As you read about transitions and the importance of moving from text to video, you'll better understand some of the transitions that have occurred. You can use this knowledge to predict the success of your own organization's efforts with video once you implement them. Consider the *how* of video while reading the following sections.

You need to know about the video styles available to your company and gain a deeper understanding of the changes that are taking place. As they happen, you can use these changes to your company's advantage. As the transition to video-based content continues, your priorities will shift to online marketing, so keep your eyes open, evaluate often, and pay attention to events as they occur. As you consider implementing your own video purchase funnel and video marketing program, keep in mind the transitions that are happening and the ways that you can easily insert video into your current activities to keep in touch with your customers.

Make keeping in touch with your customers *in a manner they appreciate* a priority goal for your marketing decisions. This is my goal for you with your own personal transition as a marketer. When you commit to this goal, you will happily implement the round-the-clock availability of online video content for your customers. These components will become part of your normal marketing day. They will also serve as reminders that your customers are embracing the use of technology and that your organization must use technology to keep in touch with viewers, and do so in a manner your customers will appreciate. Making video available has been proven to increase conversions and sales leads by other companies. Yours will be next if you'll just stick with me and learn about the following:

- ☑ The connection between the transition from text to online video and changes in the video purchase funnel;
- ☑ Great results companies have received after using video;
- ☑ Video styles available to promote your product or service;
- ☑ Common marketing activities that are happening now with the use of video;
- ☑ Upcoming text-based activities that will start using video.

As you read on and learn more about online video, keep in mind that you can use other companies and the actions they take as a model. Identifying a vertical industry and targeting your message to companies with vertical business models in that industry is something that you want to consider. It all relates to targeting your message to your intended viewers. When producing video content for the mortgage industry (a vertical market), our clients create messages specifically for that industry. This is also true for the restaurant industry, for example. There are many industries that are considered vertical industries, and crafting your message differently for each vertical industry could mean using a particular talent or way of speaking when addressing your viewers. It is vital to consider your market before you create your content.

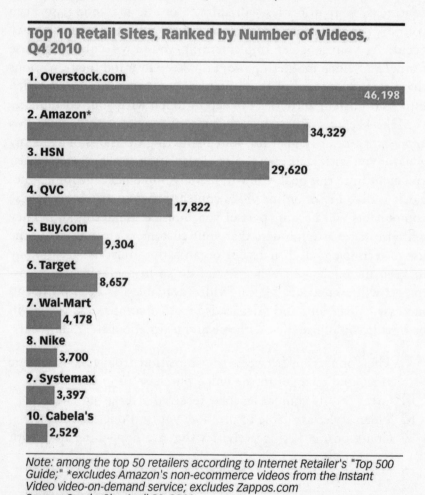

Top 10 Retail Sites, Ranked by Number of Videos, Q4 2010

1. Overstock.com — 46,198
2. Amazon* — 34,329
3. HSN — 29,620
4. QVC — 17,822
5. Buy.com — 9,304
6. Target — 8,657
7. Wal-Mart — 4,178
8. Nike — 3,700
9. Systemax — 3,397
10. Cabela's — 2,529

Note: among the top 50 retailers according to Internet Retailer's "Top 500 Guide;" *excludes Amazon's non-ecommerce videos from the Instant Video video-on-demand service; excludes Zappos.com
Source: SundaySky, April 20, 2011

127098   www.**eMarketer**.com

Figure 3.1   Top 10 Retail Sites with Online Video

Online Retail Using Video

Let's talk about the top ten retail sites. These are ranked by the number of videos produced during the fourth quarter of 2010. More than 46,000 videos were provided and available to viewers for online around-the-clock access by overstock.com. They were the major leader during that quarter for online video content. Target and Wal-Mart fell just below the halfway mark with nearly 9,000 videos for Target and just over 4,000 for Wal-Mart. These are companies that have successfully started the transition from text to video to keep in touch with their customers and provide more information about their products. It's important to realize that the shift from text to always-available video content is still in progress. Some companies have transitioned more completely or with greater speed than others.

Craig Wax, Invodo CEO, advised in April 2011 that "videos are heavily weighted toward traditional product videos. They are the ones that describe core features and benefits." This is important to note because Wax indicates that this is where retailers are starting. Why? Because they can "easily quantify the benefits," he says. There are a number of ways that you can use product videos, quantify the benefits, and reap a return on your investment. You'll read about some of the opportunities now available to you to promote your product or service with one or more online video styles. You can give each method consideration for your own company and your company's specific goals. Depending on your product or service, you may decide to produce several complementary videos to work together, or begin with one and incorporate others after you see the great results.

There are many different types of video content that can be used to engage your customers. Some are quick and easy to get up and running, while others take more planning and have a bit of cost involved in distribution. We'll begin discussing video content styles so that you can begin to create a clearer picture in your mind about the necessity of including video in your marketing plan.

Training, Educational, and How-To Videos

One of the newest ways online video influences customers is through instructional and informative "do-it-yourself" video content. If you check out YouTube, you'll find an online home for thousands of videos sharing their own how-to methods. These videos are readily available 24 hours a day, seven days a week. Customers, friends, relatives, colleagues, and prospective buyers can visit at any time. Your own organization's video content, or that of your friends and family, may already be there. When you need quick help to assemble a bicycle, make cookies for the office, plant a garden, or trim a tree, these videos are available for you. You can also find a two-second method to fold shirts, how to solve a Rubik's cube, help building an armoire, and instructions on how to kiss with passion. This is just the beginning of what is available.

"Video is increasingly important," says Justin Foster, Liveclicker's cofounder and vice president of market development. It is an important tool to "generate sales and enhance the brand," he says. "Two years ago, you would not have heard that." Your position as an online marketer is critical to the success of your company and its revenue. One of the easiest ways to start your online video education is by creating a short how-to video on your company's website. You can demonstrate your product or select a product from those that you offer. Your video will become an educational opportunity for viewers visiting your website. They will learn how to use your product, and you will have increased their trust and their likelihood of buying from you.

You can explain a service that you offer. It may complement the product that you are promoting, or it may stand alone. Explain what your company does and why. The easiest way to begin is to focus on information about your company that you can share with your viewers quickly. Speed is important. Put "create video content" on your priorities list and take the steps to get the content onto your website. These are all marketing mechanisms, the parts and pieces of a good online marketing program with video added. Creating content in video format will provide you with an almost endless method for getting your message to your customers.

Are education and training the same thing? It depends on who you ask. As you read, you'll see that they are treated as one and the same to eliminate confusion or doubt. Video content focused on training can make good sense for some customers or employee issues. Go back to your goal. What do you hope to gain? If educating customers about your material, product, service selection, or other points is beneficial to your company, then training-video content could be an asset. If you want to provide educational materials to your employees and benefit your company at the same time, it can also be done with video.

We created multiple website videos for a mid-sized company that had problems with post-sale communication. Their product was software. The benefit of the software was to make a doctor's office a paperless environment by putting medical records into a program stored online and accessed by staff on an as-needed basis. The difficulty occurred in getting staff to use the new paperless records program efficiently. Training on site helped. However, it was not cost effective, and if employees were absent they missed the material. New hires also needed to be educated from square one. The solution was to create online video content that accomplished the education and implementation goals necessary for staff to use the records program confidently. The company produced video content explaining the software, how it would benefit the office and the patient, and how to use the features of the program. They also created footage that provided answers to frequently asked questions that came up during the on-site training sessions. Staff resistance to a reduced-paper environment diminished as they became increasingly comfortable with the records program, and management realized that staff education could be successful with flexible training periods.

20 Percent Sales Increase Generated by How-To Video

"How-to" videos are used by many companies to inform customers about their products in a way that customers are familiar with. This approach is effective and has proven to increase conversions while not seeming overly aggressive. People don't like being told what to buy. They want to make an informed decision for themselves.

A lot of companies are using how-to videos on their websites to increase conversions in an inexpensive, nonintrusive way. This video style sparks an informative discussion with the viewer, rather than pushing them into a sale. A well-produced how-to video informs the viewer about a company's product and unwittingly sells the product at the same time. Financially speaking, the how-to video

Figure 3.2 Big Train

style is easy to produce and probably has greater flexibility than other video styles.

Big Train is one of America's leading providers of iced coffee drinks. The company creates how-to videos demonstrating easy-to-make drinks that customers can make at home. This video style has increased Big Train's online sales made through their website. Their demonstration videos generated thousands of views on YouTube in addition to increasing online sales during the first month the video was available.

The Big Train organization uses an episodic format for their videos. This means that they encourage viewers to check the Big Train website regularly for more video content. The increase in visits translates to more sales conversions. That's what you want: sales.

Corporate Videos

Corporate video has a specific purpose that it serves with respect to the organization it represents. You'll want to make sure you determine if you actually require an online video for your corporate needs. Remember, video content is quickly replacing text-based manuals, reports, brochures, policies, and procedures. In an organization with a corporate structure, you need to consider viewing length, purpose, and proposed content. The intent will be to engage your viewers. What's your corporate purpose? If it's training or education, double-check the education and training video section above.

"Wherever our customers are, that's where we want to be reaching them," says Alison Jeske for beauty.com. Jeske is senior director of marketing services and focuses the company's distribution strategy on "where our customers go," even if that means Facebook and YouTube. What does your audience want? These are the viewers for whom you will produce your content. Do you need to flood them with information? Do they need to be engaged, entertained, active, interactive, or to respond in some way? Who will see the video, and in what environment? Will it be noisy, quiet, crowded, dark, dim, or brightly lit? Will there be distractions or interruptions? Be sensitive to distractions and interruptions that could present viewing obstacles, especially for lengthy content.

Testimonial Videos

Testimonials are public expressions by satisfied customers who have purchased or used a product or service successfully. Respondents usually say that they will use or purchase the same product again, or at a minimum that they will work with the company again because of the service they received. Google determined that in May of 2010, a whopping 44 percent of online viewers used testimonial video content during the process of their buying decision. Nearly every website has a section devoted to testimonials. Typically it's a section of text-based kudos loaded with bland statements like "These guys are great, we'll work with them forever."

Some testimonials are accompanied by video footage. Video testimonials are much more informative and effective. When a customer clicks on a video testimonial, it actually plays a human being. The person's face appears, a title is below it for reference, and the audio allows the person to talk about a particular experience with a company, product, or service.

Testimonials like this are very simple "talking-head" videos. A satisfied customer can shoot the video with his or her computer's camera and submit it. If coordinated correctly, actively approaching customers to ask them for these videos can make it fairly easy to obtain the content. Just think about how valuable a video testimonial can be when you see the person's mannerisms in addition to their dialogue.

Some customers might be reluctant to provide a testimonial via video because they don't know how to shoot a video themselves. This can make getting testimonials more difficult to obtain. The team at greenjobinterview.com has figured out a way to get around this objection. They actually send their customers a webcam with instructions for setting up the video on their computer. They offer customer service assistance to take them through the setup process if needed. Customers are asked to film their testimonial and send back the camera in a self-addressed stamped envelope. Greenjobinterview.com has hundreds of video testimonials that make up most of the content on their site.

Review Videos

Reviews are very similar to testimonials. They might be movie reviews, technology reviews, or news summaries that are discussed by customers interested in sharing their experiences. These videos, expressing praise or dissatisfaction with products and services, pervade the Internet. No one has analyzed the depth and breadth of the opportunities this trend in online video holds for marketers throughout the world.

In a text-based world, user reviews are all over the place, and they really have changed the way companies do business. More and more, you can see these reviews starting to turn into video content. Travelocity's website contains a video from a customer who hated her experience at a hotel in Mexico. Instead of verbally ranting about her dissatisfaction with the accommodations, she took video footage of the shoddy lounge chairs and unkempt restaurant in the hotel. These videos provided viewers with an accurate description of what they could expect at that hotel.

My son is a huge fan of *Thomas the Train*, and there is a newly released show, *Chuggington*, that is trying to take away their market share. Both shows have toy trains that the kids love. All over the Web are videos created by customers that compare what is good and what is bad about these two shows. These side-by-side comparisons of toy trains and unsatisfactory hotel accommodations are just two examples of how user reviews are moving toward video, and the opportunity they can provide for you to promote your own product or service online.

Retailer Reduces Returns and Boosts Sales with Video

One 12-year-old shoe and apparel retailer focuses on online sales and service. The company, Zappos, is headquartered in Las Vegas, Nevada, and was acquired in 2009 by Amazon.com. It continues to operate autonomously. This retailer purports to be the largest online shoe retailer. Revenue in 2010 was estimated at well over $1 billion according to a case study provided by eMarketer.

Zappos began experimenting with product videos in 2009 and soon expanded the program to encompass every product it sells. It

Figure 3.3 Zappos Online Video Example

produced 57,000 clips of footage in 2010. The company is on track to add an additional 100,000 clips this year. All online video content throughout the company is self-produced. When Zappos realized that its product videos boosted online sales, increased average order size, and reduced returns, the decision was made to roll out video content for all inventory. Accomplishing this meant that the corner offices needed to ensure that workflow would be efficient and cost effective.

Big results occurred for Zappos. Williams asserts that by tracking their online video viewers' usage, they learned that in April 2010 alone, daily video views numbered 160,000. This number did not include content about their product or service that might have been viewed on YouTube, Facebook, or other online venues where syndicated clips are available. Zappos ran an A/B test of 10 percent of its customers. Half were exposed to video content. According to Williams, those who saw the clips not only purchased more but returned less merchandise.

"Probably the more significant part for us—because we're so focused on customer experience—is the fact that they were returning less," said Williams. "They were making better decisions, and when they did get the product, they were happier with it." Although Williams did not disclose a specific figure for the boost in online sales due to the ability to view video content, she did indicate that the impact was "quite significant."

Williams suggested that the sales increase experienced by Zappos was less than a prior published report citing 6 percent or more. Keep in mind that in 2010, even if the measured impact was less than 5 percent, Zappos could still realize an upturn in sales of $50 million. This figure is calculated on the prior reported annual revenue of $1 billion. Zappos, with these figures, has been able to generate profits and justify program expenditures.

Zappos intends to expand its video inventory online and offline. Soon they will also be mobile. Leaders plan to increase the functionality of social media clips shared. Williams touched on analytics and advised that they will increase the data gathered on third-party sites with respect to the video content viewed.

"We know what videos people are watching and how many they're watching a day," Williams advised, and indicated that Zappos is working to get a "better grasp" of the drop-off rates and how viewers are reacting to content portrayals by company employees.

Social Media Video

As its name indicates, this type of media is made for sharing with people in your social network. They may be friends, relatives, neighbors, or coworkers, and you're encouraged and easily influenced by the content you're viewing to, well, pass it on.

Break Media is a social media company that is very production oriented. They produce video, and they produce commercials. But these commercials are not 30-second commercials. These are videos of a longer form, and they are specially designed for the Internet. They will never run on the television networks. They will forever be running on a website, or maybe a file-sharing site, that attracts a specific type of viewer.

The spots produced by Break Media are specifically staged to run on your brand's website. They can run on YouTube and other platforms as well. The focus of the spots is that they are brand-building content; there is no intent that the video spots create sales leads or increase conversions. *Brand recognition is their sole purpose.* Advertising and marketing placement teams *want* viewers to circulate the content to others and talk about it with everyone they know. This enthusiasm is promoting their brand and creating excitement about it. When this happens, the purpose of their video content (brand building) has been achieved.

When it comes to video, you might be thinking of a 30-second commercial like those shown on television. You might still be looking at video content, online use of video footage, and promoting trust with viewers via the Internet from the outdated perspective of a television spot. This thinking has to shift.

I've found that advertising agencies and marketers need to be more willing to experiment and think outside of the television commercial mind-set. They bypass learning how to produce and deliver video content for the Web. They often hold tightly to the idea of running 30-second spots via the Internet. There is no reason to do that when you can produce ten online videos for the cost of less than one television spot. There is good news: your budget for video content will be less than that of television commercial spots.

Online Video Ad Network

An online advertising network or ad network is a company that connects advertisers to websites that want to host video advertisements. The key function of a traditional ad network is aggregation of ad space supply from publishers and matching it with advertiser demand. In the last several years, several video networks have sprung up based on the increase of broadband. Broadband makes video delivery smoother and faster. The availability of video has become much more prevalent on the Internet with broadband to serve it to viewers.

The words "video network" by themselves are media neutral in the sense that there can be a television ad network or a print ad network. Increasingly, "video network" is being used to mean *online video network*, as the effect of aggregation of publisher ad space and sale to advertisers is most commonly seen in the online space.

Performance Metrics for Rich Media and Online Video Ad Campaigns for Select US Industries, Q1 2010

1 Clickthrough rate
2 Interaction rate
3 Average ad display time (seconds)
4 Average video play time (seconds)
5 Average engage time (seconds)

	1	2	3	4	5
Pharmaceutical	0.89%	1.66%	131.65	25.45	21
Telecom/utility	0.66%	1.00%	71.01	22.70	20
Technology	0.63%	1.04%	83.78	48.61	36
Advertising/marketing	0.53%	3.90%	124.45	8.84	33
Restaurants	0.43%	0.38%	63.78	14.18	15
Travel/tourism	0.29%	2.99%	110.06	24.38	28
Automotive	0.28%	1.05%	67.14	9.95	9
Education	0.27%	0.02%	81.07	11.50	14
Finance/insurance	0.23%	2.12%	63.17	17.30	10
Internet services	0.15%	0.26%	53.40	12.32	12
Politics/government	0.15%	0.04%	92.15	11.53	24
Consumer electronics	0.14%	1.02%	63.96	9.60	20

Source: Unicast, "Analytics Benchmark Report Q1 2010," Jul 7, 2010

117726   www.eMarketer.com

Figure 3.4   Performance Metrics for Online Video

Specific industries were tracked during the first quarter of 2010 to determine where advertising dollars were being spent and if playbacks were effective. The numbers tracked only online advertising campaigns, not offline. The average video playtimes ranged from 8.84 to 48.61 seconds. The average video playtime for pharmaceutical industry videos was 25.45 seconds, yet they experienced the highest click-through rate of 89 percent. Keep in mind that these measurements are in seconds. You've got a very short time to capture the attention of your viewers and share your message.

Sales Conversion Rates Lifted by 64 Percent

Golfsmith, a 40-year-old multichannel retailer of golf and tennis equipment, began a video program in December 2009. This retailer sells brand merchandise in addition to its own products and had been dabbling in video but was not in full content-creation mode until partnering with Invodo indicates an extensive case study by eMarketer. Golfsmith's goal was to improve conversion rates for its product pages and to use video as an edge against the competition. The pilot launched with 100 videos across all product categories except apparel. Approximately 90 percent of the videos were produced by Golfsmith themselves. Their vendors produced the remaining 10 percent.

"We had to make decisions about what and who to put in front of the camera," explained Eric Mahlstadt. Choosing which products to feature in video footage was a huge challenge for Golfsmith because "we had never selected items before for video," the senior online store manager admitted.

"A golf ball doesn't really make an awesome video," Mahlstadt noted. "It's difficult to shoot someone hitting a ball," so the critical determination for Golfsmith involved the appearance of an item to viewers via video. Rather than golf balls, which are pertinent to their sales and are purchased regularly by their customers, Golfsmith elected to create a focus on shoes, golf clubs, and golf bags. This decision worked well to contribute to the overall success of their conversions. On-camera work and script preparation were done in-house by Golfsmith employees. They focused on great sellers currently accruing strong page views on their website.

Figure 3.5 Golfsmith

Successful conversion rates occurred across all product categories where Golfsmith had placed video. The test videos launched in early 2010 were tested over a four-month viewing period. No A/B testing was done for comparison. Mahlstadt said that the pilot videos got the company a return on investment at least 14 times greater than their expenditure. Evaluating the conversion increase of a particular product and matching it with overall sales helped to see this ROI in hard numbers. The next step was to check the overall increase of sales against what Golfsmith spent.

"We anticipated and measured the conversion lift, but we also received soft benefits like brand affinity and differentiation due to the presence of video," Mahlstadt explained. Because the conversion lift was "so strong," Golfsmith used other soft metrics as padding for internal campaigning. The conversion lift Golfsmith achieved met its best hopes and also increased website product views on pages where video was available. Consumer comments to the retailer were positive overall.

Video File Sharing Sites

Websites and software make sharing video content online quite easy. You can distribute your video to your viewers and hope that they in turn will share it with others. I call these *file hosting services*. Services that host video content may also be image hosting services. Social network services can now support the sharing of video. It is a bonus to their primary intention. I won't talk about them or focus on them here except to suggest to you that social networking sites can be included in your plan to distribute your video content. Future chapters will give you more information so you can confidently include video in your social network marketing and assess its results. It is also important for you to know, however, that these social network services are a natural extension and replacement of message boards. Message boards received much use and attention when they were popular and allowed their users to discuss and share information on single or multiple topics depending on the message board.

Today, social network services pick up where message boards left off and make it easy for you to post your video. Your viewers have the ability with these services to provide feedback to your company about products, services, and a sky's-the-limit variety of other topics. That's what makes video file sharing sites dynamic. Opportunities are provided through these services to share on a private basis or publicly. The filters for public viewing and comments can encompass several levels of the public outside of your company. Do you remember the old television commercials encouraging viewers to book an airline flight because *friends fly free* or to *buy a pair of shoes and get an additional pair free*? The sharing levels are similar to these commercials. When you share, your friends can be included (the first level of sharing), you can extend that sharing to the friends of those friends (the next level of sharing), and so on. Notice how there are multiple levels of exposure for your company's online video content? You want this to happen with your videos.

Multiple categories of video sharing services exist. They are usually named for the manner in which they provide sharing. For example, user-generated video sharing websites are locations to upload content you have captured yourself. Other categories include a video sharing platform, white label providers, and Web-based video editing services.

Unless you are one of the 11 percent of the population who have never viewed online video, you have had an experience with YouTube. You may dismiss this user-generated content sharing service as a website for attention-deprived teenagers with an interest in strange cats. But think about it, YouTube and similar video sharing services have the potential to change the way you communicate.

These social network websites have opened up a new channel for corporate communicators. They are part of the online revolution that will place ever-increasing demands on your organization to shift the way you communicate with your customers. You may feel excited about the changes, or you may feel threatened that they could have a substantial impact on your company's existence. Relax, I'll walk you through the important points about YouTube and its benefits to you as a delivery choice for your video content.

YouTube, the "king" of video sharing websites, is a phenomenon. These numbers tell a story: more than one-third of YouTube's users are over the age of 35, and more than 3.5 million of those are British. That was at last count, and the YouTube popularity continues to grow. YouTube has an enormous impact on viewers. In fact, YouTube played back more than 1 trillion videos in 2011. The hours of video consumed by viewers numbers 3 billion each month, and the quantity of videos uploaded to YouTube every minute jumped from 48 hours of footage to 60 hours of footage.

Tune-In Video

Tune-in videos typically occur in the lower right portion of your viewing area. This material appears on top of currently rolling telecasts of sports events and other programming. The tune-in material alerts viewers of the movie, news, game, or soap opera that will be showing next. The next show's logo appears with a widely recognized cast member of that show appearing in the same section. The message appears as a one-liner with no sound overlay. Tune-in video has replaced *TV Guide* for viewers. This type of advertising can make great sense for video.

Coming Attractions Video

Coming attractions videos are rare. Expect their popularity to increase with time and competition for viewers. The coming attractions video appears online when a visitor goes to a Yahoo! page. It may be the home page or a sports, mail, or horoscope page. An overlay appears in a manner similar to a tune-in video, described above. This overlay has a moving three-dimensional character, actor, or actress and is used to promote a show they will be appearing in soon. There is only a short line of text, if any, and the overlay is usually a ten-second maximum. After that time, it will disappear or shift to the bottom of your viewing area. There is no sound with the coming attractions video, though it is clickable and does communicate a message to viewers.

Checkout Videos

Videos are appearing more often on the checkout pages of e-commerce websites. "Check out" this great example of online video replacing text and graphics: a copier company that traditionally provided buyers with text explanations of the copy product they purchased now provides a full video description of the product when a buyer checks out and pays for their purchase.

These checkout videos are becoming more prevalent on e-commerce websites. Amazon could benefit from setting up an in-house production studio when the decision is ultimately made to provide checkout video content for all online purchases made. Right now, this vendor has a large graphics department with Mac computer equipment and a team that does graphics for their Web pages. I predict that they'll evolve, and you'll see checkout video content with every purchase you make—eventually.

Video Coupons

Have you received a video coupon yet? Video coupons aren't fully utilized with online customers to create the best benefits for seller and buyer. They easily could be. You could consider this video style for your company. Think about using an online video coupon rather than a coupon that is text based. You could make a two-for-the-price-of-one offer on a product to your customers. When you use a video coupon, your customer will click on the video icon to launch it. The coupon information will be included in the video content you provide for your customer's viewing. Your video may be solely about the coupon offered, or it may address a product or service you provide in addition to extending your coupon offer to viewers. Remember to include some "click me to print this coupon" language in your video script so your customers can bring the coupon with them to your store and receive the benefit you've offered them. I really see a move toward greater use of video coupons. It's moving, but not at lightning speed—not yet. If you're reluctant to start providing video content for your customers, this could be a good place to start because text-based coupons don't sell, but video coupons do.

Groupon and Amazon, and many traditional media companies like them, have, or will have, in-house production studios. These companies are large, have a broad base, and have a significant focus that will benefit from performing production of video coupon content within the organization. Eventually these companies may decide to accomplish this in a manner similar to their current graphic design studios. You may find that this is something that would benefit your own organization after you consider what products and services you will offer to viewers. You may in fact have so many products and services that in-house production will make sense for you.

It may take video coupons 10 to 20 years to reach their full potential. They will do it, though, because there is a huge industry attached to the outcome of these coupons. If you really consider the potential impact of video coupons on your company, you would realize the opportunity that a coupon with full-motion video could provide to your customers over an experience involving only text or graphics. To accomplish this, it will be necessary to shift your marketing perspective to include online video content for your customers. For the greatest success, launching this video style to promote your organization will provide you with easy success over your competitors.

Out-of-Home Videos

Providing video content to viewers outside of their homes is a growing way in which to establish a brand. Out-of-home video content is something you will want to consider for your own company. Why? Video content that is made available to viewers outside of their homes appears in public. You've probably seen this content style without knowing that it is referred to as out-of-home permission marketing. These videos are of varying lengths or may be a sequence of snippets. Sometimes you'll see the video spokesperson feature used with out-of-home videos. These are a few places you may see out-of-home video content: in elevators during a ride from floor to floor, in grocery stores at the checkout counter, or at gas stations near the pump you are using. The *Wall Street Journal* has placed viewing monitors in a variety of building lobby areas so that the Dow, NASDAQ, and other stock market information are readily available to viewers.

Mobile Videos

Pictures of children in my wallet are just a fond memory now. Those pictures of my family have evolved as technology has shifted. If you ask to see my son's new Schwinn bicycle, or want to see my daughter watching a Disney movie or cartoon during our drive to school, well, this proud papa is always ready—I usually show a video. Ask me, and I'll show you the videos stored on my phone. They're always ready. Some were taken just this morning because I've got the latest and greatest hot new item at my fingertips. This is a fully mobile style of video. I can have it with me and access it at all times. So can your customers, and they do.

As an online marketer, you and I are seeing a whole new concept of video-capable phones beginning to occur. The ability of 4G technology is transforming video as we know it today. This will happen especially in terms of customers seeing themselves via video as they visit with others. With the phone it has started already. The 4G will take consumers another step into video consumption. Notice that I identified it as *consumption*. The appetite your customers have for video will increase as technology increases. We talked about Moore's law and bandwidth earlier. These devices contribute to the decreasing costs associated with the delivery of video and the ease with which video can be served to your customers. These are important features to watch because they indicate the direction technology is taking—and you want to make sure your company is using it to your advantage.

Each of the phones currently available has its own specific technical requirements for delivering videos. What your company produces for an Apple device will not be fully applicable to Blackberry or Android devices. You will read more about the importance of delivering video properly in later chapters. Mobile has made the delivery of video more difficult. You need to know that a video that plays properly on a website might not work on a mobile phone. Oculu, our video delivery platform, has developed the ability to sniff out the identity of a device being used by a consumer and then serves the video in a proper format to that consumer. They may be using their device on the Web, or it may be a mobile device, an iPhone, or an Android. The Oculu delivery platform makes sure that the video is delivered in a manner their device can properly receive without distortion or disruption. There are other platforms available to deliver your online video to your customers, and I'll introduce you to several of those that I like best in the coming chapters. Remember that mobile video is happening, and it is increasingly important that you adjust to the fast-moving technology as you implement your video strategy. Delivery of your video matters, and the device it is viewed on also plays a part in how your viewers receive it.

Video E-mails

E-mails are going video. Businesses are starting to add videos to their e-mail marketing efforts mainly by creating an html graphic with a click-to-play button that opens up a new browser. The technology is not totally there yet as many marketers have found out, creating video e-mails by embedding the video directly into the body of an e-mail as you would on a Web page.

At the time of writing this book, most e-mail programs disable or strip out the video, and spam filters hate the video code. It can be done, but it's not a completely successful process yet. As HTML5 technology takes the scene, the ability of marketers to send video content via e-mail and also have that video play directly inside a viewer's in-box will increase. This feature is currently led by Apple devices, the iPad and iPhone, and more e-mail in-boxes are converting every day.

We currently see that marketers create a slick graphic e-mail message that includes a video play button. When users click on that graphic, a browser opens and the video automatically starts playing. It is a great use of the video feature in three ways. First, users think the play button is a video; second, the click-through rate in your video will go way up; and third, the messaging received via video once a viewer gets to your webpage further makes a marketing impact to increase conversions and sales leads.

Marketers and some salespeople are taking video e-mail to the next step by shooting a video of themselves and then sending it via video. The increasing availability of technology will improve video being shot from a desktop, just the person talking, or responding to an e-mail or meeting follow-up. Expanded technology will allow a video to be added to a desktop and then uploaded for delivery to an online video platform or YouTube. A thumbnail graphic can be captured from a frame of that video and sent with a link to the webpage that will serve the video. This results in the recipient of the e-mail seeing the thumbnail, clicking on it, and seeing a full video message of the message sender expressing his or her point. The potential is endless.

GPS Videos

Location-based products and services are a primary target for online video content. Advertisers wanting a national exposure and regional advertisers who want to connect with consumers in a very specific location have the capability to "serve" their advertising message to specific areas. What does this mean for your company's product or service? Take a restaurant in Los Angeles, California, for example. That restaurant can now pinpoint a particular focus to connect with customers at particular times of day, days of the week, and within certain geographical areas. Consumers who may be within five miles of the restaurant could be alerted, with a location-based video, that the restaurant is promoting a buy-one, get-one entrée special. The location of consumers is playing a large part in this new ability of companies to communicate with them via online video.

Affiliate Videos

Companies are now creating online video content and distributing this content to their affiliates. Affiliates are a feature of the Web that allows a company or individual to pay others to generate sales for them. The sales are tracked electronically, and the affiliate partner receives the commission amount agreed upon. You can use affiliate relationships as sales channels to promote your product or service.

These are similar to the soda stand at the checkout counter or the end-cap displays in a grocery store or retail environment. Here's an example: A wine manufacturer will provide a promotional display for a supermarket. This display helps to move the product into shoppers' hands and provide profit for the manufacturer and the seller. When this occurs using affiliate video online rather than an in-store display, the money that would have paid for the in-store display now funds the creation of video content to promote online sales. In essence, manufacturers produce "assets" to help distributors sell their products.

Affiliate marketing is important to highlight because this video marketing style has the propensity to increase your conversions. The onus is actually on you, the marketer, to provide video content for your affiliates. Your affiliates will then use that content to promote your products and services.

We shot a video for Vespa, a manufacturer of scooters. They ran the video on the home page of an individual's scooter website to promote them. These scooter websites sell Vespas, Yamahas, and a variety of different scooters. The videos that were produced for scooter.com were highlights of Vespa and the specials they were promoting at that time. Scooter.com ran the video as a whole-page ad on their website. Vespa in turn offered the video as an overlay to each of their affiliates who were selling their products online. Vespa actually paid for the production and delivery of the video and offered to their affiliates the lines of scripted coding that were required to properly serve the video. What does this mean? Vespa paid for everything just as you will pay for the production and delivery of your video content, a marketing asset for your "retailers" to use to promote your product or service.

You can produce video content for your affiliate partner toolkits. Marketers have relationships with their distributors and affiliates. In these relationships you can say, "Hey, look what my company has created for you. All you need to do is put a line of code on your website, and the video will play. Here is the code you'll need to make this happen. My company will pay for the video delivery. We handled the production and hope you will deliver it to your viewers."

In that scenario, let's say the video runs on over a thousand websites and plays 5 million times. There is a delivery fee associated with it, but as a marketer you keep in mind the "free" promotion that you are receiving. The video was created once and distributed via lines of code to thousands of additional websites. Your company's video played an aggregated number of video plays across all of those individual sites. That's exactly what you want it to do.

Behind the scenes of television and news media, cooperative advertising occurs regularly. It is also seen often in the offline world where companies spend money for advertisements, for example at car dealerships. You also see it in stores where companies have co-op budgets. Companies spend money on co-op media all the time. It frequently happens offline, and now there is an opportunity with online video to be able to do the same thing. What's happening offline is a model that you probably already understand. Online video can accomplish the same goal.

You want your affiliate partners to be happy about running your video content to improve their sales. Affiliate video units help to increase online sales and sales lead conversions, so be sure to educate your affiliate partners that using the content you provide will improve their return on investment (ROI). When they realize this, you will be more likely to have your advertising video run by that affiliate. Your affiliates, after you create them, can use the video content online to communicate with their customers and increase conversions. When conversions are increased, the bounty of their efforts will be received. It only takes a line of code included in their website to make this happen. It's a piece of cake to provide them with the code that will make the video play on their website and increase those conversions.

Contest Videos

Online video content is a mechanism your company can use to engage your viewers with a contest or promotion. This video style is consistent with other styles. About 10 percent of online promotions currently use video content now. Video increases the level of engagement with customers and makes it more likely that a prospective buyer will part with their e-mail address. This will allow your organization to promote to those who have shared their e-mail addresses. Accumulating e-mail addresses is the new "gold rush" of online activities.

Crowd-Sourced Videos

Crowd sourcing is one of the most effective and inexpensive ways to produce video content for online viewing, and many companies are doing it. Tap into your own satisfied customers and harness their satisfaction. Use the kudos and delight they feel in your company, product, or service as a way to create unique video content that you can use to promote almost anything. The enthusiastic information they can provide will be invaluable to your content. Contests using online video capability are a great way to attract consumers to submit their own video content for your purposes.

We often see materials submitted via video by contest entrants after it has been edited into a video production promoting the sponsoring company's product or service. The best video content received can also be used exactly as received. Both of these uses of contest video content can help you market your company's products or services and at the same time build enthusiastic support for your brand.

The ultimate purpose of these video contests is to promote a specific product or service, so announcements usually offer contestants some directions for submission. For instance, a store that sells baked goods could ask for videos of customers enjoying their coffee with a muffin or cupcake, or a mountain bike seller could request videos of a popular mountain-biking event. Companies encourage video entries by offering a prize for the best video. The winner might receive a valuable discount or a free gift for every entry submitted. Even inexpensive prizes will help to generate excitement and competitive spirit among your customers, fans, and followers. Every form of media available can be used to market crowd-sourced video contests.

Social media, press releases, and media buys are used as tools to generate traffic. It's working and changing the way businesses communicate with their customers. Examining and understanding each of the above video content styles available to your customers shows that your shift from a traditional nonvideo purchase funnel to a video-included purchase funnel is critical.

In this chapter you learned the following:

- ☑ The connection between the changes in the video purchase funnel and the transition from text to online video;
- ☑ Increases in revenue that companies have received after incorporating video in their purchase funnel;
- ☑ Video styles you can use to promote your product or service, build your brand, or create customer loyalty;

☑ Common marketing activities that are taking place now with the use of video;

☑ Text-based activities that are shifting to full video-based content.

Using text and graphics to communicate with your customers now means that you are not connecting with them in a language they expect to see in all areas of their lives. Your customers are receiving their educational and informational content via video. They are receiving their entertainment content via online video. Video is now a part of their everyday life. It is happening now, and whether or not you realize it, well, your customers do. The marketing road ahead of you is filled with online video elements that have transitioned from a text-based format to video. Video is in. And it will create a rise in your sales leads and conversions.

CHAPTER 4

Creating Video: Top Considerations for Production Success

Now that you have determined video *is* an important part of your media mix, you need to start considering what kind of video will work for you. There are three stages to video creation: pre-production, production, and post-production. It is not important for you to be an expert in production, of course, but just like you need to understand what an effective headline is, it is important to understand the production process for any online video because you will be better prepared as an online marketer to create content that will engage and interest your viewers. Production of your video content will be covered in chapter 7, but a key point is that preparation leads to well-produced content that increases conversions and creates sales leads. That preparation is happening now, while you're reading about the production stages of video. They are loosely described to give you a feel for the steps involved in the creation of your content for online video viewers. Pre-production will cover the layout of your plan from beginning to end. You'll decide what product or service to promote to your viewers and the footage length for your video, you'll work with a scriptwriter to prepare the narrative content, and you'll discuss the cast and any requirements with your producer.

During the production phase, the cast will gather with the production team to capture the action shots and dialogue necessary for your project. The location of your shoot may be the producer's studio if your product is portable and all related messaging can be presented to the production team at that location. If you've decided that a video spokesperson will work best to promote your product or service, this stage will be handled in-house by your video producer. Back at your producer's studio, the post-production stage will be handled. It is during this stage that the blending together of images in a sequence suitable to represent your product or service will occur. Music may be added or cut in with the dialogue. Additional images may be included, and voice-overs may be edited in to fit the writer's script.

The video creation process and the final video footage itself will become richer as you gain experience. The production crew at Innovate Media has had opportunities to see many mistakes that have occurred along the road to success. These mistakes have inspired the tips for online video success outlined below that you will use during your own video creation.

We have seen almost everything that could possibly happen while preparing for and executing a video project. This includes all three phases, too. The biggest problems seem to arise when the client's video in production is their first effort at online content. Give this information a good read, take notes, and write down questions, because the more you know and the more questions you ask, the more successful your first attempt will be. This chapter will help you in preparing to execute the first steps of video creation. Remember, these are not tips on how to shoot your own video on Saturday in the garage. These are tips on how to prepare for a video and what to think about beforehand to save yourself time and money. You'll learn the following:

- ☑ How the planning process is directly affected by your experience as a marketer;
- ☑ The eight golden rules of production success;
- ☑ Understanding viewer abandonment and how to eliminate it;
- ☑ Viewers abandon content that is not engaging;
- ☑ Viewer abandonment can be eliminated when you follow the rules;
- ☑ Pre-roll ads require advance planning to be effective.

As online video has evolved, the industry has come together to create a list of best practices. As you read, you will note that there

are certain things to think about before you even begin to produce your video content. Please think about your whole package
when creating a video. This means considering every step involved
from production to delivery and planning ahead for every element
required to get your content to your viewers. You'll read about
three scenarios, first a large company, then a small company, and
then a medium-sized company. No matter what the scenario, all
must consider the same issues when producing a video, and you
will benefit when you know about this information before you
begin your own video creation process.

Scenario 1—Large Marketer

Large marketers who have historically relied on television as their
primary marketing tool for drawing in customers are struggling
with creating original content and footage for their web viewers.
There is an illusion that video created for television is the same
as video for the Internet. Not so. This faulty illusion disrupts the
flow and trajectory that should naturally be found between the
two media when they work together. There is a distinct difference
between television viewers and online viewers. The two audiences
have separate habits, tastes, preferences, and styles. Using video
content created specifically for television to reach your online
viewers will not hit its mark. You may think you will be saving
money with the same product for two uses, but you are not increasing your conversions or creating sales leads, so the benefit of those
dollars you do spend are probably wasted. You will be disappointed
and unhappy with that result.

A television viewing audience has a shotgun effect. This means
that a spot run for viewers during a particular time segment is of a
"one-size-fits-all" variety. Its intent is to touch the greatest number
of viewers. Online video should be a one-to-one medium for online
viewers. The shotgun strategy is a mistake with online video. If
you are using your television ads edited down for online video, go
back to your drawing board because your content is not targeted
to the right audience.

Large marketers continue to produce TV spots to run online.
This is a disconnected formula because of the viewer targets: large
audience versus one to one. A large marketer who continues to
run their television video as online content has spent all of their

money producing television-appropriate units with no viewing units designed for the Internet. By default they play that television commercial on their websites. It's easy. It takes less effort. But less effort will not increase your market awareness and more importantly will not increase sales.

You must continue your messaging to viewers in a way that moves them to the *next step* in the video purchase funnel process. Be aware that duplicating the exact same content via television and website does not provide an opportunity for viewers to learn more about your product or service. In the large-marketer example above, television would be the first step, and the video-based online world allows completion of a sale. A viewer visiting a website can receive more communication about a product or service, with additional information beyond what the traditional television campaign offered. Web-based video, separate from repurposed television spots, gives you an extended opportunity to communicate to your viewers.

Many large companies duplicate their content. The 2012 Super Bowl is a good example. The week after the game, I was still seeing pre-roll of the exact television spots that GoDaddy, Budweiser, and E-Trade ran during the game. You want your television content to be targeted to your television viewers and your website content to be aimed directly at your visitors.

Scenario 2—Small Business Owners

Small business owners in most cases have not produced television spots before. They don't know where to start, but they do have the ability to communicate their messages with online video content for their customers. The information that applies to the large marketer also applies to the small business owner. But because there is no prior reliance on television as an advertising method, the tendency to place the television content on the Web is not a problem. The restaurant, the dry cleaner, the liquor store where you buy your lottery tickets, or the pharmacy may be the smallest retailers in your area. They have never had a reason to have video content available for their customers. They probably saw no need for video or a television commercial because they didn't have the money to buy the media in the first place.

Times have changed. The reality is that now the local dry cleaner, pharmacy, or restaurant does need a more sophisticated approach to their online presence, and we believe that video is a perfect medium for growing their business. They can easily afford to run video content via their website to communicate their message effectively. New video technology is driving down the cost of video production. It allows you, and everyone else, an opportunity to communicate your brand, product, or service in a distinct and interactive way.

Scenario 3—Those In Between

Now let's take the third situation, the middle guy between the large and small companies. This marketer simply wants to take what they are currently communicating via text and translate that into video. But they don't know how to go about it. They can't envision what a video produced for them would look like, and they wouldn't be able to create a profit-and-loss statement that would show any return on investment (ROI) that video might make for them.

The marketer for this midlevel company uses the Internet extensively for marketing but has created the traditional spots—a website with lots of text and pictures, online ads that rotate through targeted placements, and keyword optimization for search engines—but has not yet ventured into video as part of the marketing mix. In fact, midsized companies are the perfect place to utilize video marketing: the budget is there, the marketing mix is in place, and a distinct message has been created for their products and services. Budget considerations for production costs will, of course, vary due to the size and sales volume of your business. Where you shoot the footage and who you hire to produce your content will vary with your industry, product, service, and geographic location. The eight golden rules of production success apply equally to the three scenarios above, and they focus on the specific issues that you will face in achieving good production results.

Eight Golden Rules of Production Success

There are right ways and wrong ways to use video to promote your product or service to online website visitors. Some content does a fantastic job of getting viewers' attention, and some doesn't. Remember, you want your content for online viewers to:

- ☑ Engage your viewers;
- ☑ Educate or inform viewers about your product or service;
- ☑ Create an opportunity for viewers to purchase from you.

The rules are simple and easy, but they must become project priorities before any other steps are taken. These rules will always be priority, and maintaining them as priorities during the planning of your video project will contribute to great results and a pleasant experience. Using these rules will help you in getting your product right the first time, every time.

1. Keep It Simple

You are not competing to win an Academy Award. You are providing content for online viewers to increase your conversions. Keep it simple, please. Don't go overboard with the length of your video. A long-form video has a place and a purpose, and it can accomplish a purpose if that's your intent. But this is the Internet. Viewers have many priorities, they multitask while viewing, and they have other Web content competing for their time and attention. Keep your video short and to the point. Anything longer than 60 seconds and you will lose your audience. Provide them with the gist of your product or service, or an opportunity to complete a lead form for you. My clients usually want to go with longer content against my guidance, and they've found that the results aren't always what they desired. So get good results the first time by keeping it simple.

2. Quality Is Key

Professional-looking video on your site is important. Invest in good-quality cameras, great lighting equipment, and a decent editing program so that your video content will be higher grade than the stuff you find on YouTube. If your content looks like you did it in your mother's basement with her old camcorder, why bother? Amateur content makes you, your website, and your product look amateur. Yes, you can do this yourself—but you must invest in the right equipment to give your effort the polish it needs. There are also companies who create professional-quality videos exclusively for online viewing. Quality content will increase your results and your satisfaction. Professional doesn't always mean expensive.

3. *Who's Got Talent?*

Consider what demographic you are trying to reach. Think about what representative would be the best fit to speak directly to that demographic on behalf of your company. The person you select to participate in the production of your video is representing *your* company, so make sure they look the part. Whether you choose to go with the CEO of your company or hire a professional actor as your representative, all eyes will be on your representative. The message you give to your viewers about your product or service is in the hands of this individual. Video is visual content that will keep the eyes of your consumers on the person delivering your message—that person is your *talent*. Think about the late-night television ads where the car dealership owner is flashing about the screen in a silly hat or waving around fistfuls of cash. Is that how you want to portray your company? Talking to a camera in a studio with a large production crew standing nearby may look like an easy job, but if done unprofessionally it can turn off the trust in a video that was intended to inspire trust in your company's viewers. Go with talented professionals.

4. *Location, Location, Location*

Think about delivery before you start producing your video. Delivery pertains to where on your site your video will be placed, and in what format it will be streamed to your viewers. Chapter 6 will help you decide what choices to make for the delivery of your video. The best place to put your video is where there will be some sort of conversion activity, either through a sale or a form to fill out. If you can't place it there, then do the next best thing: have the video send your visitors to a place where there will be a possible conversion, such as a shopping cart for completing a sale. Delivery is the place your video will live on your website and the mechanism you will use to get your finished footage in front of your viewers' eyes. Many marketers don't take the time to utilize the target marketing opportunities the Internet offers. You will, and you'll understand how delivery contributes to the outcome of your results, good or bad.

5. Let the Script Speak for Itself

Clients who write their own video production scripts tend to go on and on and on. Repeating the same information over and over again, taking too much footage to get to your agenda, or wanting to include everything about your company in a 60-second video will shut down your viewers. They will ditch your content for your competitor's content that is engaging and keeps their attention. If you're selling a product, give your viewers information on that product only. If you want them to fill out a lead form, tell them why and ask them to do it. Continually repeating the same information, taking too long to get to your point, or overselling your product wastes time. This will definitely not get you the results you desire. Put simply, it's boring, and your viewers will not engage with your company via video. Ask your scriptwriter to set up your narrative content with these concepts in mind; then let your script do the talking.

6. Precise Video = Precise Message

Viewers aren't relaxing online with a bag of popcorn waiting to be entertained by your content. If you want to engage and maintain your viewing audience, give them the information they need to become a customer. The attention spans of viewers on the Web are short. And the more viewers who become interested in your product, the more opportunities you have for sales or conversions. When they visit your website, they are attempting to learn more about your company, your product, or your service. The video content you provide for them must give them exactly what they want: *information*. A precise video means a precise message about your product, company, or service. Decide on one item; then keep your content short, sweet, and tailored to that one item only.

7. Give Your Users Control

Many consumers feel that there is nothing worse than visiting a website that suddenly takes over their computer as if it has a mind of its own. We've all visited a website that has done this when we clicked. We were ultimately taken to a site that interested us. But out of nowhere loud music appeared, or an annoying video would just not stop playing. There were no features in place for us (the viewers) to stop the unwelcome music or continuing video content. Give your users the freedom and options of controlling the video and sound on your site. This means having volume controls, play and pause buttons, and, if your video warrants it, chapters or fast-forward and rewind options. This isn't about losing video viewers on your site; it's about creating an enjoyable user experience.

8. *Or Take Control Yourself*

On the other hand, in some cases it may be beneficial to include non–user initiated video on your website instead of user-initiated video as described above. It's really a matter of choice and what will work best for your specific website and industry. It's a good idea to run tests of your videos to gain some perspective and determine your customers' reactions. Your tests will identify whether or not non–user generated video causes your visitors to abandon your site or if user-generated video is being viewed as much as you initially estimated. A little advance knowledge will give you a lot of insight, and you will be able to use that knowledge to determine what video formats will be the best match for your customers. AARP insurance, which targets an older demographic, has seen success with non–user generated video playback as they served the video on their over-50 landing page. Viewers were requested to provide their zip code to get the conversion process started. AARP found a lift in conversions as tested against a page with a user-initiated click-to-play video.

The golden rules are important and just as necessary as under-standing the medium of video and the overall impact it can make on your marketing results when included in your purchase funnel.

Understanding the Smaller Screen

In our current world, we have to understand that users viewing online video are looking at a smaller screen, and their environ-ment is totally different from that of television. When producing a video, it's important to realize this when figuring out your message and your delivery. I can't tell you the number of times we have received scripts that look like they are written for a television spot or a marketing brochure, and they just won't translate to online video. Most users click away from these videos before they are done playing. Viewers are always seconds away from the choice of leaving your site, and it takes a thoughtful, well-designed message to keep viewers from being bored or distracted.

The concept of the smaller screen is better described as content distributed via a nontelevision flat screen. Usually the phrase "smaller screen" refers to either video delivered on a computer monitor or a mobile phone. The term "smaller screen" means so much more than just the size of the screen.

It reflects a disconnect with regard to online video. The disconnect seems to occur between the traditional advertising model and the agency model with content creators or marketers. You have read that marketers know how to produce spots for television advertising. Those spots produced for television are not always appropriate for online marketing messages. The size of the screen has much to do with how the message is displayed to viewers. Televisions with large screens deliver their messages to viewers who receive them on television or television-type technology. Ad spots made for television and delivered to online customers creates a behind-the-scenes problem for viewers because the screen size is smaller. The message is not displayed as with a larger television and this leads the customer to view the video in segments on their small-screen device. More importantly, this disconnect refers to the end user, the consumer of video, and the environment or circumstance they may be involved in while viewing a video.

Television watchers most often view a large screen while relaxing around the home. Their frame of mind is not the same as a potential shopper with a handheld device (small screen) looking to buy a product or learn more about a service. On the other hand, when your viewers are online, they can leave immediately; their attention span is shorter because they want information quickly. Viewers using smaller screens have an express mode mind-set, and it is critical that you produce your content specifically for this mind-set.

Your Viewers Have Abandonment Issues—Do You?

Viewer abandonment is prevalent on the Internet and describes what happens when viewers click away or drop from a website. The issue of abandonment is common and is a compelling reason to ensure that online media be engaging, short, and point-driven. Viewers who abandon your website video will not watch your content to the very last frame. Remember this huge challenge when working with your team to prepare a script before production.

Online viewers have *attention digital disorder* (ADD). Similar to attention deficit disorder, this means that viewers visiting web pages while online must become quickly engaged and interested in the content before they navigate away from a page. In producing your video, you'll want to consider the minimal attention spans of your customers. Television viewers are typically relaxed and ready to sit for some time during a program they've selected. Online viewing is not the same, and video production must be tailored specifically to web viewers, not television viewers. In fact, you should give consideration to the fact that you are marketing to an entirely different person.

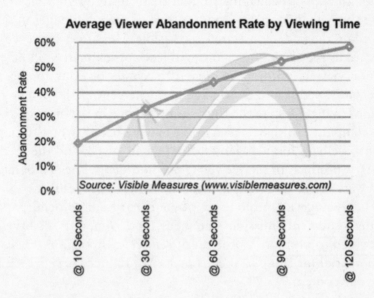

Figure 4.1 Viewer Abandonment

Visible Measures, after examining the viewing habits of online video watchers, determined that viewers abandoned more than 40 million video clips. These were unique footage spots and in aggregate have received just under 7 billion views. Visible Measures, a digital video analytics and advertising firm in the Boston, Massachusetts, area, suggests that multimedia users should anticipate losing at least 20 percent of their audience within the first ten seconds of video playback. The study conducted by Visible Measures was limited to short-form video content. This puts the time target at five-minute video clips, or 300 seconds. The loss of 20 percent of viewers as found by Visible Measures' work is a surprisingly high level of initial viewer abandonment. Wondering what this means for your own video content? Well, if your online video campaign has 10 million viewers, figure that one-fifth of those viewers watched ten seconds or less.

Viewer abandonment habits are an in-stream function of the measurement used to determine video viewing length and project results. This function can also be predicted with relative certainty given past results and research. You can see that viewing time spent decreases with the length of video content provided to view. Viewer abandonment follows a specific trajectory, and you can reduce or eliminate abandonment with engaging content that captivates your viewers.

Our own abandonment findings tend to run a bit longer in duration than those demonstrated by Visible Measures, but even so, both are in the same range. You will lose approximately 33 percent of your viewers within the first 30 seconds of your footage; at 60 seconds, you'll lose an average of 44 percent of the people that began viewing. Despite the findings by anyone in the industry, your own company will have results that may be better, worse, or equal to what we have found. Many factors are involved, and the specific industry, product, or service you're promoting and the demographic of viewers you're targeting will all factor into your results.

When you get the urge to script your marketing brochure, positioning statement, mission statement, and company history into your video to promote a product or service, think again. Focus on the potential for this extraneous matter to induce viewers to abandon your content.

Such fluff will take 10 to 15 seconds of precious video footage. Based on viewer abandonment habits and footage length, your customer will be long gone before you get to the point of your content—the product you want them to buy. Traditional marketing conversation that has history and grounding in text-based presentation materials does not always work with online video.

Abandonment Impacts Your Video Message—And Not in a Good Way

Now that you are familiar with the benchmarks for short-form video clips, you can see how effective your videos must be at maintaining the interest of your viewers. Research has consistently shown that online viewers are more likely to stop watching video and video advertisements the longer they play.

Forrester Consulting created a white paper on video viewership called "Watching the Web: How Online Video Engages Audiences." This study determined that engaged viewers make up about 40 percent of all online viewers. These viewers are more likely to watch a video all the way through, recall what they have seen, and take action. They are golden and will contribute to your success, if you use them to plan, produce, and deliver your video clips.

Tips to Decrease Viewer Abandonment

Though research shows that viewers are more likely to leave a video after just a few viewing seconds, you *do* have the power to keep your viewers watching. A well-planned video will keep your viewers attentive to your message and spark their interest in your product. Planning in advance to outsmart the statistic that 50 percent of your audience will abandon your 60-second clip takes some doing, so use these eight tips to increase the length of time viewers are happily consuming your content. Remember, the less abandonment by your viewers the better your conversions results.

1. *Clear and Concise Messaging*

Watch the length of your video. Are you bored and disinterested with the content? Your video may be too long. If the video is less than two minutes long, users are much more likely to stay engaged until the very last frame. If you think that two minutes is enough time to say all you need to say, consider shortening the length to a 60-second spot. The shorter your video and the more concise its messaging, the less abandonment you suffer from your viewers.

2. Delivery Issues

Viewers also sometimes leave because a video has delivery issues. When the video does not serve properly, it may take more time to load than your impatient I-only-have-a-minute-to-watch-this-now customer is willing to spend. Lack of planning for delivery of the footage you just produced is a major mistake marketers make. And it's within your control.

3. Know Your Audience

Do you notice that you've read quite a bit about television spots? They are a good example because the best thing about them is the manner in which they target their audience. Specific, short, and engaging goes right to that demographic. Do you see a theme here? Your job is the same, but with a different medium: online video. Specific, short, and engaging, right to your demographic. Know who your viewers will be and let your content speak directly to them with images. Hip-hop music has no place in a video targeting suburban soccer moms. Your target audience (your demographic) will determine much of what your content is and isn't. The writing style of the script will reflect the language of your target audience. So will the film shooting, narration, graphics, and editing. You will also need to consider how familiar your audience is with your company, your product, or your service. Presumably you have done some marketing and advertising before, so utilizing your existing strategy and adapting it online will help reinforce all your touch points to the target market.

4. Make It Emotional

Perhaps you want your viewing audience to cry or to laugh. Maybe you want them to learn three new things about your organization. Or maybe you want them to write you a check or sign up as a volunteer. Each of these would have a different call to action, require a different emotion or feeling in your viewer, and influence a different result. Determine how you want your viewers to react in advance; then write, shoot, and edit your project with that goal in mind. An important point about making your message emotional: do not let trying to prompt your viewer's emotions get in the way of creating a concise message.

5. Include a Call to Action

Let's face it, most viewers want to be led step by step through your website, video content, and online shopping cart feature. They will wait impatiently for an e-mail message confirming that their purchase was made and their product is speeding its way to their home. Some videos are fun but just absolutely pointless, and people with a short Internet attention span want a point—a quick one. So tell them what you want them to do at the beginning of your video. Tell them again in the middle of the content. And then repeat it at the end. Be certain to include a call to action so they will take the next step in your purchase process. When you invite your viewers to buy (or take other actions), repeat it and then repeat it again.

6. Create a High-Quality Production

Your consumers viewing online video will probably be fairly lenient when it comes to the quality of your video and audio. In fact, many viewers are drawn to sites like YouTube because of the amateur, authentic video content that hits them *right there*. Oh, and you'll need to hit viewers with your content *right there* if you want them to act on your call to action. Stick with quality, because if there is an annoying buzz in the audio, if the sound is out of sync, or if the video is pixelated, your viewers will move on to a different video— and it will probably be your competitor's. Your quality doesn't have to be created by a professional with multimedia production expertise. But it should at least be good. Take some time to learn proper lighting techniques and shot framing if you plan to create the video yourself. Educate your employees if you intend to create an in-house production studio so that they will produce a higher-quality product. Quality doesn't always mean out-of-the-ballpark expensive. Your video is really an extension of your brand. It will represent your company, so do not let poor quality content reflect in your customer's decisions not to buy. Do what it takes to produce professional content. Your viewers will thank you for it, and you'll smile when you see your conversions.

7. Use Talent to Your Advantage

You read about the eight golden rules and using the proper talent in your videos. This is important and bears discussing again. You can use talent to your advantage. Oftentimes our clients want their CEO, an employee, friend, or family member to act as their company's representative in video. As discussed earlier, being in the spotlight looks easy, and when it comes down to brass tacks, this decision, if not reconsidered, can skew the appeal for viewers, insufficiently engage them, increase your drop-off rates, and decrease your conversions. This is not about having 15 minutes of fame. This is ultimately about the end result your organization desires and taking the explicit steps necessary to get them. In more than 95 percent of productions, hiring the right talent is critical to the success of the project. The talent must suit your target audience, have personal appeal for your projected viewers, have a natural ability to express passion for your product or service, and share that passion with your viewers in a believable manner. Resonating with viewers is paramount to the successful outcome of your footage. Testing your talent will also help you determine whether viewers are responding to them and to what degree. You'll read more about this below, in "Testing ... One, Two, Three." The impact created by your talent, no matter who that may be, will determine the effectiveness of your video. If you're all right with spotty results or a less-than-desired return on your investment, put your CEO in front of the camera and take your chances. But you picked up this book for a reason. You wanted more information, guidance, and the ability to maximize your results and your ROI, right? So think twice who you'll invite for your talent, and stick with the best choice to create the best ROI.

8. Testing ... One, Two, Three

Determining the overall value of your message, your talent, and how they are working toward your video's ROI will require some online testing. You do this by measuring the impact of your videos on conversion, sales, and ROI. Then you can optimize performance by an A/B video test to determine the optimal production and presentation style, length, merchandise, or any other parameter. We will get into this in greater detail, but do not let the importance of testing overwhelm you. While we were working with Service Magic on a particular video production campaign, it was important to determine what video actor was creating the most conversions for them. We shot five actors reading the exact same script. Three were male actors, one with dark hair, one younger, and one a little bit older wearing glasses, and two were female, one blond and the other brunette. One of the actors was already familiar to viewers who signed up for a free 30-day trial because the conversion (result desired) was that viewers sign up for that free 30-day trial. We served the video campaign and broke it up five ways to send traffic to five identical landing pages. The differentiating feature was that each actor read *the same exact script*. We were only testing to determine which actor drew the most conversions for Service Magic during the script read. Because the demographic was heavily slanted toward males, we were convinced that one of the females would convert the best. Guess again. There was a clear winner, but it was not either of the females. The winner was the older man with glasses who created an 18.5 percent conversion lift off the same landing page as the other actors. That conversion rate exceeded all of our expectations.

Pre-Roll Units

Customers frequently ask me for guidance in using video as ads for online promotion and how to use their video in upcoming ads. Pre-roll has become the place where a number of video plays are occurring on the web. You will read about the pros and cons of using it in several sections of the book, depending on its purpose. Pre-roll behaves much like a television ad. Viewers are provided with footage in 15 or 30 second segments before they can access the content they chose to see. This type of ad unit is creating an entirely new set of challenges for online marketers. You will want to take a shortcut and use a television spot you already have running and use it in your online creative arsenal; please do not. You are probably asking yourself why we are talking about pre-roll in the chapter about creating video. It is important that you create video specifically for your pre-roll. That begins in the creating and

planning process of your video content. It is vital that you understand that using your television ad online will not serve your company in the best manner possible. This means that repurposing an
existing television ad into an online video spot will not produce
the results you want. You will be disappointed. It will not work
effectively for reasons already stated, including (again) that your
pre-roll must target your audience in order to lift your conversions
and create the ROI you have estimated that it can create.

If pre-roll advertising is so dominant, why should it change?
Industry colleagues agree that changes are needed. Cory Kronegold's
blog, *Why Pre-Roll Advertising Should Be More Interactive,* discusses
that online viewers do not want to passively watch an ad; they want
to be able to engage with the content moving on the screen in front
of their eyes. He also confirms the broken model of pre-roll.

Although pre-roll advertising currently dominates, approximately
45 percent of viewers abandon the content they intend to view when
it is accompanied by pre-roll. This is important to note when producing your own content. Also, with a 0.1 percent click-through
rate, pre-roll engagement is low. A change in the status quo is
needed to balance the discrepancy between the high use of pre-roll
ads placed by advertisers and actual engagement by consumers.

A change in the status quo begins during the production process
of online video while the creating and planning phases are in full
swing. If you are a marketer producing a television spot, consider
planning an extra day of shooting with all of the actors and cre-
atives present. You can produce additional content for your online
viewers that could compliment your television spots. You might
shoot a slightly different version of the spot you will be running on
television or a completely different version. Whatever you decide
to do please remember that your pre-roll guidelines should follow
the same things discussed in this chapter. The viewer of pre-roll is
in a different environment than the viewer of a TV spot. You must
take that into consideration and target these distinctly different
viewers when you produce pre-roll. Your pre-roll will also become
more effective when it is created specifically for those viewers who
may be using smaller screens.

When you are planning your pre-roll, you can work toward getting highly specific during the production process. To do this,
consider creating your pre-roll content from the keywords your
viewers will search for to get information about your product or

service. Oftentimes, content of onsite videos that we create for clients also includes the pay-per-click keywords they purchase via search engines. You have the same opportunites.

Jeremy RedGrey suggests that, "Pre-rolls are re-purposed (television) except nobody watches them." This means that if an environmentally minded viewer watches online video content about saving polar bears, the migration of penguins, the devastation that occurred during the Louisiana coast oil spill, or the fulfilment of a child's last wish, that viewer is presumed to have an increased propensity to view pre-roll pertaining to something similar. You would not want to show this viewer pre-roll for John Deere tractors, airline promotions, home improvement ideas, or clothing content. The likelihood that this viewer would abandon your video is greater when your content is not specifically aimed at this customer. It is critical that you recognize the point being made here and how it relates to your own organization because it directly influences how you market to your customers.

Pre-roll, if you choose to use it, must be short. RedGrey says, "If your media plan calls for a 30-second and two 15-seconds, SHOOT a 30-second and two 15-seconds." Your content needs to be less than the length of the shortest typical television commercial. Short means short. The structure you will be using to develop content for television speaks directly to viewers who are relaxed, committed to spending their time at that moment to watching a particular show at the convenience of the networking station.

Online viewers are not of this type. You must create content specifically for them and serve it to them whenever they choose to view it. Use one message per pre-roll or video and make sure that the message is presented in such a way that your viewers will be captivated by it from start to finish.

Pre-roll is just one form of video that you may produce and deliver to your viewers. You learned much information in this chapter to assist you in creating online video content for your company. You now know how to engage and target your viewers and the steps you need to take. Here is a quick review of those top points for you to remember:

☑ The planning process is directly affected by your experience;
☑ The eight golden rules of production success will make your project a success;

☑ Viewers abandon content that is not engaging;
☑ Viewer abandonment can be eliminated when you follow the rules;
☑ Pre-roll ads require advance planning to be effective and are not your repurposed television spots;
☑ Viewers do not appreciate disruptive advertising messages.

Your success with online video will be directly related to your perception of these concepts and how thoroughly you implement them. Viewers who visit your website for more information about your product or service have an expectation of what they hope to see when they click on your site. Remember that your video will require advance planning in the production stage so that you do not offend your viewers or contribute to viewer abandonment. Make sure that the rules, all of them, are on your priority list and receive the attention they deserve. Your viewers are depending on you to make their online viewing experience satisfying.

CHAPTER 5

Return on Investment (ROI)

This is the chapter you wanted to read first, right? Maybe you started with this section and figure you'll make it through the rest of the book's content when you have more time. You should make money on your videos, and this chapter will highlight ways to do that successfully. You should also be able to easily cover the cost of your video production and the delivery of your content. When production is done right, you will have properly executed the rules and put the tips into full force during production; these steps alone will contribute greatly to your return on investment (ROI). But ROI is not about the money. The ROI of placing video on your website for online viewers is about increasing your conversions—the sales and the sales leads. The ROI flows in from these sales and these future purchases. When your video is done properly, there will be a return on the time, energy, and money you put into the production, not just on what you are spending on the marketing side of it. In this chapter you will learn about the following:

- ☑ Which video formats to use to get your content in front of your customers;
- ☑ How to measure clicks, impressions, views, or visits;
- ☑ How and why testing your video can increase your sales leads and conversions;
- ☑ How to measure your customers' viewing and abandonment points;
- ☑ Exploring video's other uses.

ROI—The Necessary Ingredients

When we hear clients say to us, "We tried video and it didn't work," our response is simple: "You did something wrong. The script was too long, or the copy was wrong. Maybe the actor didn't connect. It could be that your video wasn't delivered right." Video works. We know it, and we have stacks of analyzed case studies that demonstrate video's success at creating conversions. You want a return on your investment, and you'll have that return when your production is right, your actor connects, your video delivers smoothly to viewers, and your script is concise and interesting. Each of these factors plays a part in laying the foundation for the success of your online video. These are the ingredients your project requires. You need sugar, flour, salt, baking powder or soda, eggs, chocolate, and other stuff to make and bake a moist chocolate cake. Without the necessary steps to make it so enjoyable, well, it won't be. Video has steps to create success, too.

You need to think about two components of online video when it comes to creating a positive ROI or increasing conversions: production and delivery. You'll read the details on those topics in a later chapters. They are the key variables when determining your ROI, and considering them during your initial conversations about the video campaign and its production will enhance your profitability. Key questions to ask when starting your first video project:

1. Should we produce the video ourselves?
2. Should we hire a video production company?
3. Should we deliver the video ourselves?
4. Should we place the content on YouTube or use an online video platform?

These are great questions, and you want to be thinking about them *now*. Yes, ask them, and know that they will be answered in the following pages because they pertain to your ROI and will affect your outcome. Web video can deliver a higher ROI than paid advertising's traditional methods of banner ads or PPC.

MediaMind suggests that online viewers remain longer on sites when the ads are included with video. The increase in dwell time is estimated at 100 percent. When you make creating collaboration among your marketing efforts a priority, and this includes online video and any television commercials you may decide to run, you will be supporting your brand loyalty and awareness. Video is known to increase brand recognition, and brand recognition is important to your ROI.

In August 2010, ComScore's research indicated that "the cross-platform viewer is more receptive to advertisers' messages than a TV-only viewer." This finding is important to the ROI of online video. "Cross-platform" means that a product or service message has a collaborative effort going on in both online video and television broadcast commercials.

Data were gathered to examine the categories of interesting, enjoyable, memorable, favorable thoughts about brands advertised, and whether viewers stopped watching a television program to visit an advertiser's website online. The percentages were higher for cross-platform viewers than for those who watch television only. This presents interesting information for online marketers who are using, or beginning to use, a video-included purchase funnel.

A study was conducted by Nielsen in April 2010 to determine the effectiveness of advertisements. The metrics of the study included recall of ad, brand, and message. Messages that run as a television ad *and* as an online video gain better viewer recognition than a single-platform message. And this equals ROI. But the important thing to remember here is that this refers to "message performance" running over both television and Internet mediums. This is not, repeat *not*, a video made for one medium and rerun on the other medium too. Your mediums must be separate. The message you provide for your viewers may be the same, but your medium must be specifically designed for the viewers intended. Television viewers are one audience; online viewers are a separate audience. The two do not mix. Your media efforts must complement each other in ways that each of these two audiences expect to receive information from you.

Show Me Some $$$

Let's look at some numbers for a hypothetical company. Their online marketing budget is $100,000. Of that amount spent, they received 100,000 clicks to their website's landing page. On that landing page, they have one product listed at a per sale price of

$100. Currently, they get a 2 percent conversion rate. This means that for every 100 clicks to that landing page, they receive two orders or $200 in sales. The 100,000 clicks that they've received with their marketing budget of $100,000 yielded 2,000 sales. Two thousand sales at $100 each would make their ROI $100,000 because they spent $100,000 to make the 2,000 sales. But they do not have video on their website's landing page.

That same company could add video to their page and increase their conversion rate by 20 percent. You may think this is out of the question, but case studies and data indicate that this is true. In this circumstance, their conversion rate would increase from 2 percent to 2.4 percent. Following the same scenario above, the 100,000 clicks at a 2.4 percent conversion rate of 2,400 sales at $100 per sale would equal $240,000 in sales. Sales just increased by $40,000. But what about production costs, delivery costs, and all the other associated expenditures? Well, if the production of the video costs $3,000 and the annual cost to deliver the video on that page was $500, then the video initially costs this hypothetical company $3,500 for an increase in sales of $40,000. They will spend about $500 each year to maintain the delivery of that video and continue converting views into sales.

In the above scenario, the company initially increased sales by $36,500. It's important to put this into perspective. Simply by adding video to a landing page, they increased their revenue. If you're a marketer creating a television spot, you could spend $100,000 to $300,000 or more on just one television commercial. You can, and should, take some of that budget to create online video content during the same filming session. Currently most online videos connected to television shoots are produced in one of two ways. Either the efforts for the television spot take most of the time and almost all of the budget, or the television and video shoots are done on two separate occasions and are not connected. You want your strategy to include both features, produced at the same time. Your online video can be produced during the same filming session as a television commercial. When you produce them both during the same session, you'll have content to capture viewing audiences in both media. Your budget won't increase because you're splitting it between both media, and your content will increase your conversions and ultimately pay for itself.

Running online video that is merely a repurposed television spot reduces your opportunities to use specific video formats that are known to increase conversions. There are three formats you'll consider for your project, and your producer can help you decide what will work best for your company. I'm convinced that if done right, video will increase your conversions. If that's the case, your investment in video production and delivery should be a good one.

Testing Your Video

Practical Ecommerce found in November 2008 that merchants such as Archie McPhee experienced increased conversion rates averaging 30 percent, with a range from 12 percent to 115 percent. Testing of video results is done in a manner called A/B testing. Think back to the example given in the eight tips to decrease viewer abandonment. We tested video for Napster using five different actors who all read the same script. This is an example of an A/B test. There are a number of ways to test your video, and the aspects to assess can include the representative, script content, colors used, and music incorporated.

Landing Page Optimization, by Tim Ash, suggests that testing be done to determine your current conversion rate and whether it is hitting your estimated mark. Some testing methods will need to be conducted by your information technology department if you choose to use software designed especially for testing. Ash suggests that if you don't have a landslide of conversions each day to measure, then other features should be measured.

Ash addresses optimizing landing pages that are text based. Much of his testing for text-based pages can be reworked for testing of video. Make testing work for you by ensuring that it is easy to design. If testing is not easy for you to design, do you think you'll use it? Do you think you'll use it regularly with each campaign if needed? The easier your testing is to design, the more likely you will be to use it. Implementing your test must also be easy. If there is much to set up, many departments, software features, or steps to follow to begin the testing, delays can crop up and shift your attention elsewhere. Ensure that your test will be easy to analyze. You won't need 30 reams to review to find your benchmarks if you set up initial testing with basic features. As time goes by, you can always add factors to test and increase the time that you run the testing. If your test is not quick and easy to explain, go back to the drawing board. Testing needs to be simple—simple to plan, simple to execute, and simple to understand. If it's not, you'll have problems the minute you begin.

But what do you test? Decide how many versions you want to split your test into. You may decide a 50/50 split or a 33/33/33 split would be appropriate for your test. The traffic coming to your website would then be directed to each split page equally. One will eventually be a winner, that is, after you decide the length of the testing. It could be 24 hours, 72 hours, a period of 30 days, or some other time factor you decide upon.

You can give yourself some flexibility in the features you test. You might test headlines, subheadlines, or light and dark colors during one test, background music during another test, and a variety of scripts in a subsequent test. If desired, the layout of your page as viewers see it or your call to action could be tested during future splits. These features can also be tested in cases where you don't have many conversions at the beginning of your testing phase. They can help you gain conversions as you continue running the video for your website viewers.

Testing Tips for Better Conversions

Testing is common online, but most marketers don't test video. You should include video in your testing activities. You should always be testing. Ash, a landing page conversion guru, urges testing to increase conversions. If you haven't noticed yet, when a company tests, they are letting their customers decide what converts best. Then they keep it up to keep their customers happy—and buying. Your company may already be optimizing your website and tracking conversions, and you may already be conducting A/B split tests of your landing pages. Do the same with video. Optimizing your video content creates an impact on your conversion rates with a simple A/B video test. The easiest and quickest way to do this is to take a landing page or checkout page and serve that exact same page with the video and without the video. The better performer will be apparent from your conversions. After you see an increase in your conversions, you can try the following types of video A/B tests.

Test Talent against Talent

If your video content includes actors, see which ones perform best by testing them against each other (there is always a clear winner). You can do this in a way similar to how we did our testing for Service Magic. Each actor will read the exact same script. That's the test. It's easy, it's quick, it can be tracked, and it can be split. This simple test will show a winner. If you really want to stretch, test multiple actors against each other at the same time. This means you'll be shooting more than two at the same time. When you test in this manner, you'll have the footage done without extra time or expense in the studio. As I mentioned above, one will always convert better than another, and you can never determine in advance which one is the best fit.

Shift Wardrobe Colors

Just as you can test different colors of art, graphics, text, or background on your landing pages and lead forms, you can do the same with the color palettes on your video or on the actors in your videos.

Script vs. Script

Long script content can be tested against short scripts. Different copy can be tested by your hired video talent, the voice-over, or your walk-on spokesperson. As with the copy on your webpage, your customers will respond differently to different messages.

User-Initiated vs. Non–User Initiated Videos

One of your decisions to make during planning will be whether or not to let your viewer have control of the video. This is one of the eight golden rules and has advantages and disadvantages. Testing user control of your video will give you good benchmarks for extending future control and the conversions it will bring—or drop. User-initiated video requires that the viewer click on the play button to start the video. This does impact your conversions, and you'll read more about it.

The truth is that the only way you can expect to improve your video's performance on your website is through a meticulously implemented optimization program based on consistent execution of A/B testing for all the variables one can tweak on one's site. A/B testing is extra work, but it's worth the effort when the results can increase conversions. The extra work involved with A/B testing requires that you have at least two versions of the site element that will be tested. The site element might be the text, design, image, buttons, video, color, or music. Your framework will need to be effective for planning, implementing, and evaluating your test results. Sadly, this additional effort is enough to make the majority of e-commerce/lead generation site operators decide to give up on the entire exercise.

Numbers Won't Lie about Conversion Lifts

My experience in the industry has taught me that nearly all marketers A/B test their marketing initiatives but not their videos. Without A/B testing, it's simply impossible to isolate which elements of a page provide better performance and by how much. Occasionally the results gained from this type of testing will prove the exact opposite of what your own gut instinct may tell you; but that doesn't change the fact that the result you got is based on cold, hard data. And that data is precise and actionable. If you're not implementing A/B testing on your site now, you'll never figure out what exact elements of your site are providing you with the highest value in terms of ROI. It takes a bit of work, but it can be simple and easy with a little effort. Resolve yourself now to test, test, test—and make sure your testing includes video.

Do Your Viewers Measure Up?

Online video analytics is a way of measuring how viewers get to an online video and what they do when they watch it. Oftentimes, online marketers don't even think about video analytics, and they should. Looking at the analytics available for your video content will enable you to evaluate whether or not your viewers measure up. It is similar to checking your website analytics to see what visitors are doing on your site. If you've got video, get your viewers measured up. The analytics for your online video will tell you the answers to questions like these:

- How long did viewers watch a particular video?
- Did they watch it to the last frame?

- Did they abandon the video? If so, when?
- If the video is user initiated, did they click on the video?
- What was the video's click-through rate?
- Where did the viewers come from?
- Did they click through from content that was related to a particular topic?

If you choose to deliver your video content through an online video platform, your service provider will provide you with detailed analytic data. The data, as you read above, can show you how viewers interacted with your video. For example, one of the key pieces of data we look at is called video completes. The video completes stat tells us how many people watch the video to the last frame. If we check the video completes and find a very low video completion rate, we know something is wrong with the video and your viewer is not relating to it.

Measuring online video presents both challenges and exciting opportunities for marketers—challenges because of the time involved in testing and evaluating analytics, and exciting because you can see precisely what a viewer did with the video content you served on your web page. Reviewing the metrics provided by your online video platform (OVP), if you choose to use one, will reveal both how your video has spread virally and how your audience engages with your content. Get familiar with these metrics; they are industry standards, and you'll discuss them with your OVP-provider and multimedia producer during the planning phase of your video.

Use Different Types of Measurements

Web analytics is the act of distinguishing categories within recorded stats and analyzing them for patterns. This process of analytics will disassemble the whole video-viewing process so that you can study each component. Web statistics programs have various methods of tracking and measuring important criteria related to the viewing of your video content. These criteria include visits, visitors that are unique, and views of your pages. Keep in mind that you want to compare and measure like with like for best results. Always be sure your analytics program can give you the information about your viewers that you want and need to ensure increased revenue.

Sometimes it's not easy to compare the results generated by two statistics programs while tracking one website. Thinking through your needs, comparing the different programs available, and deciding what you will measure are good exercises and useful to execute. But consider using several different programs. We encourage the use of numerous programs, for example combining a tracking service with log analysis.

If the method of measurement stays the same through time, then the results will be perfect for purposes of comparison. So, choosing the method of measurement is important. Scientifically speaking, changing the method of measurement during an experiment invalidates the process. Make your decisions in advance, during your planning phase, and stick with them for best results.

If you compare results from two types of measurement, you will find differences in numbers. Measuring page views versus unique visitors, for example, or the whole website versus specific pages gives you an idea of what it means to compare results from two types of measurement. From these examples, you can clearly see that the numbers will not be the same. If you compare the same statistics over time, you will avoid changing the method of measurement. This is the most accurate way of recording statistics. This method will allow you to find patterns and definitive answers, and you can readily see if your traffic is growing or diminishing. You will be able to determine whether your campaign to generate new leads is working and whether your visitors are returning to your website again. Your efforts to bring targeted traffic through a PPC campaign to create conversions will be achieved, or not, and you'll know through measuring, just as you'll see in cold, hard data whether your returning visitors generate more revenue than first-time visitors.

What to Measure

In any statistical endeavor, the first step is to define what is being measured. In website cookie tracking, the common denominator is human events, clicks on a website, which are defined as page views. Specifically, the statistics discussed here are a translation from raw data, clicks, and server-browser dialogues into a user interface from which patterns can be recognized. The goal of web metrics is to extract patterns that indicate what is happening when your visitors arrive and view your page. The next step is to take action to make the best use of your traffic patterns.

Web metrics and analytics are an exciting field at this moment because there are not many patterns being studied. An example might be comparing "bounce rate for first time visitors" with "bounce rate for returning visitors," which has not become a standard of analysis yet. Measuring these would provide aggregate bounce rate stats to indicate how far into your site your visitors are clicking.

Real-Time Stats and Ongoing Fine-Tuning

Trends are aggregate statistics. For example, a Web's bounce rate is an aggregate statistic. Bounce rate is a metric designed for the purpose of identifying patterns that are hidden within the statistics. Discrete statistics such as click streams will tell you what individual people are doing on your site. But discrete statistics are not aggregates, as you are actually seeing what comprises the data.

Click stream analysis is very useful for development purposes and for understanding viewers' reactions and use of your site. If you are designing a new site, knowing how first-time visitors navigate will help to determine how successful the site is, and what changes may be required to increase sales leads and conversions. As Web-based video becomes more prominent and more useful for businesses, the biggest issue is figuring out what resonates with your audience. Keeping a close eye on your numbers after you post a video will help you know if it is being watched to the last frame. The numbers you review may indicate that your content is too long or not engaging, or that it is well liked. The delivery mechanism you choose to stream your video will have many tools and indicators for you to use so you can increase your conversions.

Basic Video Analytics

YouTube is the first place many start. YouTube is great for beginners to video analytics. It is easy to upload a video, share it across your website, and collect some very basic traffic statistics too. But you get what you pay for. You can see gross viewership by day, some demographics (age and sex), how they got to your video (via organic search or some other website), and so forth. This is a good starting point, and certainly better than nothing.

You also have a timeline of the video that shows you when someone stopped watching, or when they hit the rewind or fast-forward buttons to get an idea of how they were or weren't engaged in the video itself—this is shown by the color of the bar graph for each visitor. You can see how your viewership declined during the run of the video. With some videos, you can lose more than half the audience by the time the last frame is shown. The longer the video, the larger the drop-off can be, which is why the average video is getting shorter and shorter.

No matter which service you use to host your videos, you need to study these analytics regularly. You have to spend some time with the analytics pages for each video you post and return to the pages on a regular basis (such as once a day, week, or month) to see what is getting watched and what isn't. This helps you figure out what your audience is interested in, what portions of your video aren't engaging your audience, and how you can make your next video more of a hit.

Online Video Platforms

Having an online video platform allows you to enjoy a report that does the viewer tracking for you. A report of this nature tracks how many people have seen your video, how many viewers watch the video to the last frame, how many clicks the video receives, and the actions that a viewer takes from the video. Data packages are available that easily plug in. Most video producers are stationary, so your video will serve itself from a fixed location after it is set up. OVPs are also delivery systems that help you manage your video inventory. You may create one video soon and many more over time, and an OVP's organizational capabilities will support you in keeping them all managed. You'll know what video is where and the viewing numbers on it, and all of your content will be stored in one place, not in various locations throughout the Internet. An OVP will make managing your video a task that you'll look forward to handling, and the organization of the system will support anyone taking on this job. Organization will also contribute to your overall understanding of how effective your videos are. You'll know what is coming from where, when it does so, and what it took to get it there.

Other analytics an OVP can provide for you are via syndication because online videos travel from site to site and viewer to viewer. As they do, they spread and change in unpredictable ways. Once viewers find your videos, they can vote by clicking their mouse while the video is in playback mode. Then they can rewind it to rewatch the parts that captivated their interest or that played while their attention drifted. Your metrics reveal both how your videos spread virally and how your audience engages with your content.

Viral ROI

In the current video age, nothing goes viral without some social media coming into play. When it does, most viewers need to be moved or motivated beyond the norm in order for them to put something in front of their friends and followers. We have not talked about this much and won't go into details. But since we're on the topic of ROI, it is important to touch on it. You've noticed through the previous chapters of this book that viral video is not our focus. It can happen and it did happen regularly before big shifts occurred in the Internet. Our discussion is focused on ROI. And yours should be too. New clients often ask us to "make a video that will go viral" for them. That is completely doable, but first we need to identify what they mean by viral video.

What makes a video go viral? What triggers the act of sharing a clip on Facebook or Twitter? How do these shares affect your ROI? It's not enough to create pretty images or great special effects if your audience doesn't feel anything when your video is finished playing. Return on investment for a viral video clip via social media marketing and advertising is hard to determine. The added benefits of viral and social media marketing are not consistently quantifiable, and without firm analytics to see if the benchmarks were hit, we cannot quantify the results.

The initial stage in figuring out the ROI for viral video and social media advertising is defining achievable targets for the campaign. These targets are achievable ambitions for viral video and social media advertising, such as enhancing subscribers, followers, and supporters. This stage describes the aim you'll have of developing an increasingly growing base of online influencers and customers via social networking websites.

Attain ideal video views. The number of desired views is primarily based on the approach, investment, and channels utilized for distribution. Decisions need to be made with respect to targeting national and global views, and the impact they will have on creating conversions.

Boost web-page traffic. Subscribers, supporters, and followers must be engaged frequently by the use of social networking. Your videos will contribute to engaging them and creating their desire to stop by your company's website and learn more about your products.

Enhance consumer engagement and interaction. The time viewers spend with your brand and the purchases they make contribute to your final result of enhanced revenue.

Enhance conversions. Improvements may be required to enhance conversions. Soon after converting viewers, analysis and evaluation can determine what steps may be necessary and what percentage of complete views is achievable. Conversions can show the largest increases when videos address viewers' attitudes and behavior.

Reduced advertising expenses. Promoting your product or service over a long period of time as viewers receive it from others or find it on the Internet can support a viral strategy that will reduce advertising expenses.

Improve bottom-line income. This is usually the top priority for most companies. Outlining price points and developing strategies for achieving those goals must be created right after defining your marketing campaign and the results you expect it to produce.

On social networks and video clip-sharing websites such as YouTube, users' online lives merge with their real lives when videos, posts, and tweets appeal to them. Their interest is typically concentrated and receptive simply because they are choosing to view the content (opting in), escalating the probability of message retention and enhancing the value of the advertising subject material.

The individual nature of video and social media marketing and advertising tends to make for a far more qualitative assessment in terms of ROI. To maximize this benefit as a marketer, make sure you define the strategies you will use to obtain your objectives.

These strategies must include the production of viral content, establishing relationships through engagement, and increasing your product or service's Internet presence via the use of additional tools.

Purely organic viral advertising requires a sufficient amount of time exploring targeted channels on social networks and video sharing websites. Your spending budget needs to involve media fees if you want to venture into that marketing and advertising venue, and your budget should contain the cost of someone's time if you are heading the purely organic route.

The moment you have implemented your viral video clip and social media marketing campaign, stay on track by means of analytics or other monitoring tools. Immediately after your marketing campaign has concluded, or has been moving along for a designated time period, ask yourself if you achieved your benchmarks. Hopefully your answer will be a hearty yes and you will have earned positive ROI. There it is again, that increase in revenue.

Who Will Control the Video: Non–User Initiated vs. User Initiated

The eight golden rules suggest that your viewers should control the video content you serve. But keep in mind that it can be non–user initiated content as well. Think about your website and consider these factors that could increase your conversions. How your customers are presented with a video will affect your ROI. When your customer comes to your site, the video can automatically play (non–user initiated), or the visitor can click a button to make the video play (user initiated). This is really important, and it is something that online marketers rarely think about. You want to consider who will have control early in the planning stage of your video. If you want to be aggressive with your videos, you'll serve non–user initiated content. If you want your visitors to check out your website, look at your content, relax, and think about whether to buy from you or not, you'll want the user-initiated content style. With this style your viewer can look at your video, or not, at their leisure.

There are a number of factors to think about when making this decision. If you were to shop for a new car, you might meet two salespeople, one passive and one aggressive. The aggressive salesperson would walk to your car with purpose, meet you there as you open your car door, shake your hand, welcome you, and begin to show you around while at the same time exploring your interests and preferences for a new vehicle. The passive salesperson would stand near the door or sit at a desk in the showroom, welcome you when you approached with questions or to ask for help, shake your hand, and begin to show you around.

The energy and tempo demonstrated by the two salespeople are very different. You would react very differently to each of them. Your preference may not be that of your friends, colleagues, coworkers, or customers, and their preference may not be the same as yours. Just like the two salespeople have distinct styles in selling cars, you will develop a style for your company or organization too. It may be passive and user initiated, or it may be aggressive and non–user initiated.

Keep in mind, however, that research shows that at the end of the day the salesperson who meets you as you step out of your car sells more cars than the salesperson waiting for you to come into the showroom. They both have the same script; their script has the same message. But that annoying sales guy moves more products on a monthly basis.

Now, ask yourself how you will execute video control on your website. Our numbers tell us that the non–user initiated video helps your page convert better; almost 100 percent of the time the non–user initiated video performs better than the user-initiated video. Are you surprised?

You'll need to walk a fine line if you provide non–user initiated video and greet your customers when they visit your website and deliver your message to them. While some enjoy it, others will sit there hoping for it to end. There could be a problem. You might receive complaints that some of your customers find the non–user initiated video annoying. Most online delivery platforms offer some sort of tracking cookie for your videos. If you decide that the non–user initiated style would be best for your needs, you can include a cookie on your website, and the video will only appear once for your viewers.

Let's go back to the car dealer analogy to help you address this "annoying" issue. The manager of the car dealership has to deal with the 10 percent of complaints from potential customers who are annoyed by the aggressive salesperson rather than providing support to the salesperson waiting in the showroom who has only average sales. As an online marketer, you'll also have that line to walk. You might get some complaints from customers that the video is annoying. The issue really is about making more sales while knowing that the annoying video works to increase conversions. This is also true for the video spokesperson overlay and the embedded video content.

Remember, and this is key, if you have a user-initiated video, the best-case scenario would be that 15 percent of visitors will click to play the video. And that means that 85 percent of your customers will not see the video because they did not click on it. If we know that a customer who watches a video will be more likely to convert, won't we do everything we can to make sure they watch the video? Is it worth annoying some of your customers to make sure all of your customers watch your video? I don't know the answer to that for your organization, but it's a key question to consider when thinking about the ROI for your videos.

Other Ways to Get a Positive ROI with Video

Other than conversion activities, there are a lot of ways you can save money with video. You don't want to get offtrack here, but as you plan your video content and your online video purchase funnel, think about including video content to provide ROI from various video styles. You've read and want to remember the following:

- ☑ Which video formats to use to get your content in front of your customers;
- ☑ How to measure clicks, impressions, views, or visits;
- ☑ How and why testing your video can increase your sales leads and conversions;
- ☑ How to measure your customers' viewing and abandonment points.

Increasing your revenue is what this is all about. ROI is the reason we produce video, upload and deliver content, and help online marketers create these same great results for themselves. Online video has truly transformed the way that content creators and audiences engage, share, learn, and collaborate.

If your video doesn't pay for itself, then you won't use it. You'll have the best success when you produce it after you have a distinct basis for measuring your ROI. The simplest way to measure ROI is to decide what you want your video to accomplish and see if it's being done. What are you trying to increase and create a video specifically for that objective? What message are you trying to deliver? Only when you identify your communications objectives can you identify the returns you're likely to get from the implementation of video.

Chapter by chapter you have read about online video evolving from a relatively promising, one-way mass medium into a popular and far-reaching platform for delivering engaging, online user experiences. Since the very beginning, marketers and merchants have been looking for ways to monetize video content as a method for achieving ROI; some have succeeded and some have not. In the early days of this industry, the blocking-and-tackling of ROI concerned the most effective ways to monetize and measure entertainment content through advertising strategies. Today much of the content we see is informational and carries a vastly different value proposition.

As for the ROI metrics themselves, they tend to align directly with an organization's specific business priorities. Sales will prioritize revenue generation, marketing and PR will focus on global reach, and executives may place greater emphasis on productivity gains. In a recessionary economic environment such as this, however, the ROI debate remains fluid.

In addition to positive payback—a conversation we may not have been able to have just a few years ago—the growing community of users and vendors has learned a tremendous amount over the past decade about the role of live and on-demand web video in business communications. By understanding that online video solutions remain vitally relevant, you can quickly put your department or organization on the path to capitalizing on the full potential of video.

No longer viewed as "emerging" technology, tools for creating, managing, distributing, and measuring video content have matured to the point that we enter our second decade in a business climate where online video is not only widely accepted, but also expected.

Using an OVP with analytics capability is an ideal way to track your campaign's success. You'll have real-time intelligence that will allow you to continually optimize your campaign and ensure that you receive the highest ROI possible. The OVP and analytics will give you a real idea of how much traction your online video campaign is getting. Video ROI equals increased revenue.

CHAPTER 6

Delivery

Production and delivery. Delivery and production. These two strategies go hand in hand. Oftentimes companies produce a fantastic video project without giving advance thought to or planning how that content will be delivered to their viewers. Serving and streaming are also terms used in the industry that mean delivery.

Delivery matters because when you produce an outstanding video and fail to think forward about the delivery of that video to your customers, well, their user experience is reduced. This can contribute to or be a cause of viewer abandonment. Smooth delivery plays into your viewers' experience of your content, and your content represents your brand, your product, and your service. You do not want to blow your opportunity to increase your sales leads and conversions by shortchanging your video delivery. Much is riding on your decision to plan your delivery in advance. In this chapter you'll learn the following:

- ☑ Delivery is as important as production in the online video equation;
- ☑ Delivery options are available to get your content in front of your viewers;
- ☑ Free-delivery-in-exchange-for-ads providers (like YouTube) are not your best option to serve video on your site.

Online video delivery platforms are available to deliver your video and provide you with the analytics necessary to determine your conversions and sales leads.

In 2006, Dave Winters and I connected and developed an online video production company. Ninety-nine percent of our business at that time was strictly in producing video content. Our services were limited to pre-production, producing, and editing. When we had the digital files finalized, we sent them to our customers who in most cases were marketing executives. We had absolutely no involvement in the delivery of the video. Eventually we needed to distinguish our business from other video production companies. Dave and I realized that we needed to offer delivery services to our customers, and that we could do this by creating a technology platform to serve video. We began working on the development of Oculu, and now when a client comes to us to produce video content for their online viewers, we can offer them extensive service.

Three Video Formats

Video can be delivered via the Web in only three formats: overlay, embed, and lightbox. It is critical that you understand these delivery formats. Master an understanding of these three mechanisms so that we can help you realize the increased conversions your website has the potential to receive.

Figure 6.1 Overlay

Overlay

You have experienced overlay at some time during your own Internet experience. The overlay format is when a video just overlays on the page. You can put it in different areas of the page, but the point is that it fundamentally lies on top of your Web page without any need for specific space to be devoted to it. This format really works well when you already have a webpage developed but you don't have time to work with your tech team to place the video in a certain location on your page.

Embed

Probably the most common format used to insert and stream video through Internet web pages is by embedding it. The embed format requires that you have a specific space on your web page to place the video. The standard embed size we use is 640 by 360 pixels, so your Web designer or Web developer will need to adjust the material currently on your site to provide specific space for the video. This represents the amount of space required to adequately operate the video. The advantage of this format is that your video will look really good on the page, and it will allow your page to flow seamlessly with the

Figure 6.2 Embed

video. A problem can occur if your website was already designed and in place. You'll need space to place the video on your site. If you decide that the embed format will work best for your company, give consideration to the size of the video and where it will be installed on your web page and plan accordingly, in advance.

Lightbox

Last, but not least, is lightbox. Lightbox works off of a click—for instance if someone clicks on a graphic or a click-to-play video on your page. The video will then launch, and the sides of the video are either blacked out, red, or something along those lines. The lightbox follows the same rules of an overlay where you don't really need a specific space. I like the lightbox for specific activities, but not for conversion activity. Once the lightbox launches, your viewers are not able to click on the page, or anywhere outside of the video. This means that if you have a lead form and you have a lightbox video, your viewer cannot actually fill out the form while the video is playing. The lightbox is a great format to use when you want your viewer's full attention on your video content as it pops into the viewing space in front of their eyes and engages them. The lightbox also does not take up any space on your Web page since it pops into view, so it can be a great solution when you want viewers to "click here to play" or you want multiple click-to-play videos available.

The delivery of your video to viewers can be planned in advance, and the format selection you make to place your video on your

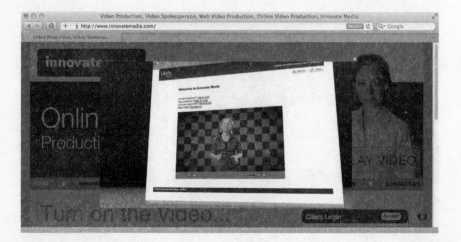

Figure 6.3 Lightbox

website will affect the location of the video and the ease with which your viewers can see and receive it. This is the first issue you must consider when you begin planning your pre-production phase. It will make a world of difference to the outcome of your video when you always ask yourself: What format will I use to deliver my video?

Delivery

Production and delivery are very different processes; they are the yin and yang of online video. Production requires a combination of art and science. In production, there are people in front of and behind the camera, and someone editing the footage that gets shot. Delivery is technology and is more coding and programming than art. It requires someone to know an entire list of programming language. Unfortunately, as more and more devices hit the market, delivering video properly has become more complicated. Producing and delivering are two totally different skill sets. Keeping this information in mind, consider the following question which will impact your project: How will I deliver my finished video content to viewers online? You have three options:

1. Self-delivery—You can give your video files to your tech services department or your webmaster and let them figure out how to get the content to your viewers.
2. Free-delivery—You can deliver it on a free-to-use user-generated content (UGC) website such as YouTube. Remember that these sites are free in exchange for serving their advertisements along with your content. For the purposes of our discussion, we will put all of the UGC sites under the category of free video services (often referred to as YouTube).
3. Online video platform (OVP)—You can use a paid hosting service that serves and manages your videos for you. A variety of OVPs, along with their advantages and disadvantages, will be discussed in this chapter. The appendix will also provide you with a list of OVP providers that can customize services to your needs.

Let's define what I mean by delivery. The terms "delivery," "serving," and "streaming" are used interchangeably but actually mean something slightly different. "Delivery" is often used in reference to a video when it is being served to viewers. All videos you produce will ultimately be served, either by your website or through a third-party server, and that third-party server may be free (UGC) or fee-based (OVP). Not all videos get delivered to their final destination, though. When they do, this is considered to be video complete because the content made it to your viewer's eyes and ears. You will be able to see how many viewers experienced video complete and how many abandoned the viewing content when you review and evaluate your analytics. Your biggest goal as a marketer is to have your video delivered properly.

The critical issue in delivery is that your content plays correctly while your customers are watching it. It's that simple. There will be nothing worse for your company than producing a video that perfectly communicates your message only to have it frustrate viewers because of poor delivery. If the video takes time to buffer and your customers are required to wait while it does, they will abandon your video. That's why you must think about delivery as much as you think about production and your ROI if you want your online video execution to be successful.

Many cases exist in which companies have spent a lot of money on the production of their video without thinking about delivery. One case that comes to mind had their tech team build a playing system for the video. The video played very poorly. This company's message and future communication with abandoned viewers was lost, probably forever. Other issues that contributed to their poor delivery and unsatisfactory viewing experience included the following:

- Viewers couldn't hear because the volume on the player was preset to a very low level.
- The video did not play automatically (non–user initiated), so viewers had to sit and wait for it to load.
- No feature to close the video was included for viewers. Typically this is a button labeled with X or "close."
- The video was served as a flash file, so it did not work on most mobile devices.
- As the video was loading, it was competing with other elements on the web page to load first.
- The lightbox format was used, and the player was not displaying on the Web page correctly.

- The player was set up as one size fits all and gave viewers no controls to enhance or personalize their viewing experience.
- The video only worked with the Internet browser version it was initially set up for and did not work with that same browser after browser updates were made.
- The audio and the video were out of sync with each other.

Above are only nine reasons that video can deliver poorly, and the experience can be unpleasant for viewers. There are many more reasons, but the point is that delivery is critical to the overall success of your video campaign.

Free Delivery vs. Fee Delivery

The decision that the marketer needs to make is whether they are going to deliver via a free service or a fee-based OVP. The available free delivery services are primarily YouTube and Vimeo. The fee-based OVP services number more than 60 choices. Both free and OVPs offer the option to insert embedded video in your blog or website. They will also deliver your content to mobile phone technology. There are a number of free video-hosting services, but YouTube and Vimeo are the most familiar to readers by name. All free video services come under this category.

Free Delivery

Be advised that YouTube is not your best option for video delivery on your own website. It is a better option than trying to figure out how to serve the content to viewers yourself because delivering video is difficult. But you do have options besides YouTube. If you decide that you want to deliver your video yourself, or that your company wants to create its own platform to serve the content to your viewers, select YouTube instead. YouTube, though, has trained online marketers who are using video that their service is better than choosing other delivery options. At some point YouTube was the only option available, so this made sense. But times have changed dramatically.

Using YouTube as the delivery mechanism for your online video content should be your plan B. But please don't think that it is your only option. Choosing an OVP to deliver your video for you will make your experience more satisfactory and will provide optimum viewing conditions for your customers. Yes, the OVPs are fee based. Yes, you'll spend some money, and this will increase your overall production costs. But your ROI will also look better when you evaluate your analytics.

A small company may decide not to engage an OVP with a large server base to stream their video content to their website. But as video drives more sales, it is important to reevaluate this strategy regularly. By using an outside professional firm to handle the video content delivery, there is no worry about capacity issues that occur with respect to accommodating graphics, content, and video without upgrading to a bigger server. The small company that chooses to deliver via a free service is also taking on each of these problems and must correct them in-house. Big Train created success with the strategy presented earlier. When we began working together with them as a vendor, they had a lot of video content on YouTube. They were actively using the YouTube player on their site to serve video. Together we shifted their delivery, and they no longer use YouTube to serve video on their site. They use an online video platform that has performed well for them. Big Train doesn't have a lot of cross-platform video content; the videos they are hosting on YouTube don't appear on their site and vice versa.

One can argue that YouTube is sufficient to act as a video server. There are considerations pertinent to YouTube and other free services that are critical to your delivery decision. YouTube appears to be free. It is not. There is a price to pay. Free services like YouTube make their money by serving advertising messages to their viewers. In some cases, your company, not paying a penny for your service, must be willing to share screen space in front of your viewers with advertising messages promoting other companies' products. Your company makes its money by selling your product or service. I'm not suggesting that you boycott YouTube. YouTube can contribute to your online video presence and provide your company with benefits. Remember that you want YouTube and fee-free services as additional OVPs for your video. Your primary OVP that serves your content on your website should promote and benefit your brand, not its own brand.

Partnering with a free service to deliver your video content really won't be a symbiotic relationship for you. Some of the actions YouTube takes can conflict with those that are best for your business and your marketing goals. While YouTube has a very good streaming quality and is on the forefront of delivery and serving technology, customer service and conversion suffer. Here are some reasons why a marketer might not want to use YouTube or other free services to deliver your videos on your website:

- If you use the YouTube player, it might carry the YouTube logo on your website. Do you really want the YouTube logo to load in your brand if you have no choice or cannot disable this feature? You could spend the extra money to have a customized player that displays only your brand.
- YouTube may serve related video content after your video has completed. Recently one of my customers (an eyelash makeup company) wanted to produce and deliver a how-to educational video. We produced the video to their satisfaction, and they turned to YouTube to deliver the video on their site. Here's what happened: once the video ran, YouTube served eyelash-related videos on their site, and those advertising videos included our client's competitors. Though not by choice, this company promoted their competitor's makeup product by selecting the free service that YouTube offers. The cherry on top was the display of their competition's related and recommended videos offered to our client's customers. What an uncomfortable experience.
- In some cases, YouTube will serve ads on their player. You probably do not want ads promoting other companies, their products, or services while you are marketing your own product. Obviously the ad serving is an issue for your delivery unless your company doesn't mind promoting your competition.
- YouTube is great for video search engine optimization (SEO), but for the online marketer, there are some issues. A Google search could pick up your video content even though YouTube is serving it. The search engine that is searching will find the video, but the viewer will be directed to YouTube to watch it, not to your company's website. If your video is being served on your site, when search results locate your video, viewers will be directed to your website to watch the video, not to YouTube.

- You want viewer clicks to move your prospective customers closer to your company and your website. If your video SEO strategy is to send traffic to your video on YouTube, thank yourself for helping Google sell their ads.

Large companies block YouTube on their office computers. We see big companies blocking UGC and social media sites. Facebook, Twitter, and ESPN are several examples of blocked websites; there are many more. From a business perspective, this makes good sense. These companies do not want their employees wasting valuable office time interacting with these sites when business is the priority. YouTube is a website that has a propensity to be blocked by large companies with regularity. If you were trying, for example, to get a video viewed on your site using the YouTube player for workers at Target, Wal-Mart, JCPenney, or Macy's, and those companies block YouTube, your video will be blocked, and *it won't even play on your own site because of this blocking.* And it brings up the point of mixing business content with entertainment content, so you want to add this to your list of delivery items to consider.

The last thing YouTube wants you to do is leave their site. The only thing you want as a marketer is to have viewers go to your site or stay on your site to buy your products and services. Remember the intent of the parties involved with free-delivery video: YouTube sells advertising; you sell your company's product or service. They may blend together or separate like oil and water, so determine your marketing objectives, set your priorities, and move forward.

YouTube's technology is incredible, and I'm not knocking it or other available free services. They have done a wonderful job convincing marketers that self-delivery via their service is the first place to start when they want to upload and stream video content. From a financial perspective, the price is probably right for many businesses, and I am challenging you, the marketer responsible for your company's brand, customer loyalty, and market recognition to think differently.

The bottom-line recommendation you'll receive from me is to use a professional fee-based OVP and expect great results. If you choose to use free services like YouTube, create a strategy for your video placement. Here are my suggestions. You'll notice that to accomplish them, and for greater ROI from the strategy, it will be necessary to do the reverse of what you think is best.

1. Plan your delivery strategy and video content.
2. Produce your video.
3. Deliver your video to your website first.
4. Develop your own video SEO strategy.
5. Syndicate those same videos to all the free video-hosting sites.

Fee-Based Professional Delivery

Online video platforms are mechanisms available to stream your video content to your viewers through your website. By definition, an OVP is typically a software-as-a-service (SaaS) solution. The SaaS provides end-to-end tools that you can use to manage, publish, and measure your online video content. An SaaS solution supports both on-demand and live delivery.

Typical components of an OVP include video hosting, encoding, custom players, syndication, and analytics, as well as interactivity and monetization through a variety of online advertising options, typically third-party ad servers or networks. Ultimately, they allow website visitors to receive minimal buffering. This is accomplished by adapting the quality of the video stream in real time based upon your customer's changing bandwidth. You want this for your viewers because it means that the start-up time for your video is fast and they won't have to wait for your message to load.

"With the recent glut of online video platforms—more than 60 of them and counting—organizations face both unprecedented choice and intimidating confusion when it comes to the best way to get their video online in a way that will help them grow their business," says Eric Schumacher-Rasmussen, editor of *Streaming Media* magazine. The market for OVPs has expanded rapidly. They are becoming increasingly focused on a wide array of capabilities that include content management, encoding, advertising, syndication, and monetization.

Most of the larger OVPs were developed for publishers rather than organizational marketers wanting an online video presence. As the market further expands and more choices become available, you will want to ensure that you remain at the top of the information curve. Keeping up with the technology will help you to make better buying decisions for your company, understand and integrate the newer solutions, and select OVP choices in a saturated market that provide the best benefits for your organization.

Optimal execution of video play at the moment your customer or potential customer wants to watch your video is critical. You do not want to leave this important element of your delivery to a free delivery service, or to your tech team unless they are experts in video delivery. An OVP can be worth the cost and will pay you back with increased revenue on the back end.

Advantageous Online Video Platform Features

There are a number of video platforms on the market, and each offers multiple features with different pricing structures. Some of them have feature overkill, and you probably will not need everything they offer. There are ten core features that you need in an OVP. Keep in mind that you'll read about ten features below, although there are hundreds of features available depending on the vendor, capability, and technology involved. This list is targeted at you, the online marketer. You'll want to explore several OVPs and compare features, price, and how they satisfy your needs. You can find cost-effective solutions that will help you deliver your content; you may just have to put in some effort. These ten features will also help you know what you don't need in an OVP.

1. Video Management—The best and most important feature of an OVP is the video library management capability. You can reduce your video workload when you manage all of your online video content in one central location. The platform should offer all the tools you need to organize your video content. Uploading and encoding your videos is part of the management process, so make sure the upload video tools are quick, easy, and allow batch uploading.

2. Multiple Play Options—We have discussed the three video formats that make video delivery over the Web possible. Any good OVP should offer the overlay, embed, and lightbox formats, as well as provide the code or script necessary to easily insert on your website.

3. Ad-Free Solution—Many professional OVPs have the capability to serve ads in the videos they are delivering.

Remember, you're an online marketer, and you don't want to serve ads in your videos, or at least you want to have the option not to serve ads. You want to use your videos to market your products and services, so make sure the system offers a way to serve videos without ads. Be aware that some delivery pricing models are based on serving ads.

4. Analytics/Reporting—Analytics are a great way to monitor your video's performance with viewers, and most OVPs offer Web-based analytics. Again, a lot of the analytics packages out there are overkill, and some don't apply to the marketer. You will want features that include video plays, click-through rates, viewer abandonment information, viewer engagement, unique searches, and social video play data.

5. Scalable Serving—Most OVPs serve from content delivery networks (CDNs), and as a customer, you should not have to worry about the scalability of your video plays. It is the OVP's responsibility to make sure your video is playing properly and that they choose the correct CDN. Make sure that the OVP you choose can provide scalable video delivery on demand for your videos without risking quality, reliability, or delivery times.

6. Custom Players—Player solutions should be logo free. They should preserve and enhance your messaging and brand. Be sure the system can "skin" the player to match your company's website and your corporate "look and feel."

7. Video SEO—Most OVPs have an automated SEO feature that will allow you to create site maps by video title and submit them to the popular search engines. Your video can then be used to bring visitors to your website. One way to get search engines to view and rank your videos is through a solid video SEO strategy.

8. Video Syndication or Social Video—As you've read, we believe your best bet is to start your video on your website and then develop and implement a strategy to incorporate the social media sites like Facebook, Twitter, and YouTube. OVPs usually have great syndication tools, and they will allow you to automatically syndicate via their management platform. One click of a button, and you will instantly distribute your video.

9. File Formats for Mobile Devices—There are multiple delivery options out there, and you want to be dead certain that your videos can be delivered outside of flash on such devices as the iPhone or iPad. Any good OVP should provide this capability and also address mobile video delivery. Many include detection technology that can identify the device your viewer is using to watch your video. Videos should deliver seamlessly on any device via an OVP.

10. Live Support—You deserve prompt human access to the video platform team when any issues arise. Technology in the online video publishing industry is changing quickly. Make sure that your solution can grow with new technology developments and bring new features to market in a timely manner.

Devices Make Delivery Complicated

Online video delivery is no easy task. The presence and variety of mobile phone technology, HTML5, and the ever-changing browsing community are all contributing factors to the difficulty. *Video Compression for Flash, Apple Devices and HTML5* by Jan Ozer provides further guidance for incorporating online video delivery with mobile devices. "The production and distribution of streaming media has been complicated by new playback devices like smart phones, new codecs like WebM, emerging standards like HTML5, and new technologies like adaptive streaming." There are resources that discuss this topic because it is so important and so vital to the smooth availability of video in the organizational marketplace. As the online marketing community continues to expand to promote more products and services, additional knowledge will be critical to reduce the burden of getting your message to viewers via mobile devices. From the perspective of serving quality video to your viewers, this information is significant to point out. You may, or you may not, have trouble due to mobile technology issues.

Brightcove's CEO Jeremy Allaire has noticed that the emergence of new technologies has helped business. "People thought HTML5 was going to be a panacea," he advised. As it turns out, HTML5 provided publishers with challenges when they work across various platforms to accomplish their service of video to viewers. "It's been one of the greatest sources of new business for us," Allaire reported.

Future websites will be built primarily in HTML5. Also known as h264, HTML5 does not support flash, and as of this writing, popular opinion suggests that flash usage is becoming obsolete and moving toward HTML5 as the new standard. This shift is a major transition. Steve Jobs sort of started it by not allowing flash on iOS for Apple devices. Right now the most important aspect of HTML5 support involves serving video on those iOS devices. This can be accomplished in two ways: via browser or via iPhone or iPad. Delivery services, both free and fee-based, have built-in watchdog technology to detect whatever device browser your viewer may be using, and this detection will help you get your video streamed.

Analytics/Reporting

You have already read about analytics and the need to evaluate various reporting features that pertain to your video and what your viewers do with that video. These bits of information ultimately help you with your viral marketing. The delivery mechanism you choose will have a definite impact on the analytics reports you will be able to receive. The free delivery video services will provide you

Figure 6.4   Oculu Online Video Platform: Analytics Data Dashboard

with limited analytics, while on the other hand, the OVPs have extensive analytic packages.

At the very least, most OVPs will detail your video views and report download bandwidth. They may also provide details like the country and domain of your viewers. Beyond these basics, many OVPs also present true viewer analytics that allow you to identify patterns within the statistical data. Reporting data is truly important to you as an online marketer. You have many delivery options available, but a professional OVP will serve you well and build your brand or product awareness without free-delivery logos or ads. There are hundreds of other variables available to support you in analyzing your video's viewing data.

The reporting dashboard demonstrates a feature that is provided by many OVPs. The dashboard in figure 6.4 shows you that video starts are tracked and can be evaluated against complete video viewings. The completes are occasions where your viewer sat through your video content all the way to the last frame. Oculu, the OVP service used for this dashboard example, also shows time frames, viewer quantity, stops, completions, and click-through actions taken during viewing. When selecting your OVP, you will want to ensure that a feature similar to this dashboard is available so you can track and evaluate your own viewing activity.

Video Starts

A video start is simply how many times your video has started playing. Most analytics packages consider a start to occur after the very first frame of the video plays. Measuring the start of your video is very important because it is the base measurement for all other pieces of data you will evaluate.

Click Through

All videos are clickable, and you should encourage your viewers to click on your videos with a call to take an action of some sort. Your click-through rate (CTR) can be improved when you modify or make changes to your video. Some of our customers suggest a click during the narrative of the video. You can do this as well when you have your representative or on-screen actor give viewers a "click on me" instruction.

Figure 6.5 Oculu Viewer Abandonment Chart

The chart above, titled "Engagement Report for G&G iAd script 3", reads:

This report tells you when your viewers stopped watching this video.

% of video watched	0-10	11-20	21-30	31-40	41-50	51-60	61-70	71-80	81-90	91-100	Total
Yesterday	652	48	47	29	24	24	42	31	35	890	1822
Last 7 days	4989	770	533	475	452	477	464	491	561	9584	18796
Last 30 days	21816	3409	2536	2335	2167	2382	2317	2426	2862	44242	86492

User Played

One of our customers noticed that their user play data was about 1.5 percent. They were not really happy because this mean that about 98.5 percent of their viewers visiting their website were not watching the video content available to help them better understand the products and services. In this case, the video was delivered as user initiated, and viewers could choose to watch the footage. User-played data via OVP is important to evaluate because it will demonstrate whether or not your users are playing your user-initiated video, or whether they are abandoning your video when it plays automatically. Information about these issues is good, and it helps you to make adjustments for better results during the next tracking period; it also helps you analyze and understand your conversions.

User Stopped

This data relates to non–user initiated video content. When your video starts playing, it will track and tell you how many people stop the video after it starts. Your viewer must push the stop button to cease video streaming. Using the user stopped data can help you determine if your videos are annoying them.

Video Completions

Video completion charts provide excellent data in the form of drop-off statistics. These numbers are critical to your conversions because they identify for you exactly when viewers stopped watching your video. If you have massive drop-offs within the first 30 seconds or so, you have the data to back up recommendations—even if one of those recommendations is to ditch your CEO's greeting. If few viewers make it through to the end of your four-minute product demo, you know that you need to get to the point more quickly, or perhaps present that video later in the sales cycle. Viewer abandonment is measured in seconds. Zero to ten typically equals the percentage of a video that a customer watched during particular time periods. Measuring viewer abandonment will help you to know if viewers leave your content, at what point they leave, and if there is anything you can do about it. Charts and a variety of tools are provided as standard OVP features for easy evaluation of your video content and its results. The chart in figure 6.5, by Oculu, gives various benchmarks for playback review. No matter who your OVP provider is, make sure you have this assessment tool included with your service.

Video Platform Providers

If you decide that you will use a professional fee-based OVP to serve your video content, plan to research and interview several providers. Some are better suited for online marketers than others, and each has their own twist and particular orientation. For marketers and merchants choosing an online video platform, attaining the correct balance between the technology platform and production quality can be difficult. It may require serious investment across multiple suppliers and in-house operations. The appendix at the back of this book contains a list for you of what I feel are the best OVPs for marketers. There are many that can get your video streamed to your viewers, and you will need to check them out yourself.

So, remember the highlights of this chapter. There are three video formatting options and plenty of resources for delivery of your content when you want high-quality, fast streaming for your viewers. Delivery is critical to your online video conversions. No matter what you choose, remember, nobody thinks much about delivery until it's time to get that footage to viewers and problems arise. When you think about delivery and make it a priority now, your product will surpass your expectations.

In this chapter you learned the following:

☑ Delivery is just as important as production in the online video equation;

☑ You have options on how you choose to deliver your video;
☑ There are a number of online video delivery platforms that you can use to deliver video;
☑ YouTube might not be your best option for serving video on your website.

Let me say it one more time before you leave this chapter. Delivery is critical to your video's ability to increase conversions and generate sales leads. This is not something you want to take shortcuts on. Make each step a priority and walk them in sequence: delivery, then production—think backward! Now that you know why delivery is vital to generating revenue with online video, let's move on to the production of your video content.

CHAPTER 7

Video Production

As big as delivery is, production is equally important. We went into detail on the delivery component of online video in the last chapter, and now it's time to cover the intricacies of production. But first things first. I need to point out that this chapter is not a how-to guide for producing Internet video, with detailed information on what cameras to buy or lights to use. There are plenty of books out there that can be used as resources for your self-production education. Instead, this chapter will focus on production experiences, including mistakes I've seen other marketers make. These insights will help guide you through the video production process. You'll learn the following:

- ☑ Production options available to help you create your video content because, like delivery, you have choices that include self-production or professional production;
- ☑ The roles and goals of all involved in the project;
- ☑ Music selection for your project;
- ☑ Why you may need to attend the on-set filming of your project;
- ☑ How the green screen technique can reduce your production costs;
- ☑ The pros and cons of hiring a production company or filming yourself;
- ☑ Tips for a successful production;
- ☑ The process of a typical video production project from beginning to end.

Production Tips

Video produced properly entails a lot of moving parts and can be costly to produce. Price shopping is not the best approach. Remember, sometimes you get what you pay for. There is always going to be somebody out there who will produce your project for less, but really see what each production company will provide for you. Go into your initial meeting with a checklist of what you want, a list of questions, your marketing strategy, and the language you have created for other mediums.

See if the production company you are interviewing really understands your company, your product or service, and your strategy. Finding a good partner will benefit you in the long run because unorganized video shoots are a complete waste of your time and money. Preparing well in advance will save you headaches and cash. Here are seven critical experience-based tips to remember when preparing your video:

1. Location-based shooting is expensive and can cause problems. Sending a crew out to an office or to another off-site location should be considered during the budgeting process. In some cases it makes more sense to film in a studio where you can have your crew, talent, and equipment come to you.
2. When on location, you do not have as much control as you would in a studio. Sound and lighting, for example, can be affected because you are in an unknown environment full of unwanted variables.
3. Shooting in a studio, especially in front of a green screen, makes good sense for online video production because it offers greater post-production flexibility.
4. The cost of an entire production day is high even if you do it right. If you don't have a gigantic budget to work with, creating the proper situation of "lights, camera, action" for just your company may not be feasible. You can hire a production company that will scale your costs by shooting for multiple clients in one day. This could be a money saver for your project.
5. The single most time-consuming element on a production project is editing. For a production company, this is where the cost is a huge variable. Sitting someone at a Mac to create motion graphics for your video project can take a lot of

time. It can also spiral out of control if not managed properly. Understand before you begin how much editing and special effects are necessary for your end product.

6. Not all graphics are created equal. The more graphically intense your video is, the more time it takes an editor to produce it. Therefore your video is a more expensive production to create.

7. Always rent equipment if you can; don't buy it. For example, if you plan to self-produce or produce in-house, don't buy a $60,000 camera. Rent it for the days you need to shoot. That camera will be obsolete in two years and will never pay for itself unless you somehow manage to use it every day.

The Production Process

Let's take some time to look at the entire video production process. If you can master and understand these steps, you will become a lot more efficient at making videos, whether you are doing it yourself or hiring a production company to do it for you. Regardless of what role you take, you'll be involved in all the elements of production from start to finish. The one thing I learned early on was that videos are actually built from finish to start. This means that many of the steps you would think occur at the end actually take place at the beginning of the process. Below is the order in which the steps of producing a project occur:

A. Pre-Production

1. Project concept, goals, and schedules
2. Scriptwriting/storyboarding
3. Asset gathering
4. Hiring talent
5. Production variables

B. Production

6. Shoot day
7. Equipment and crew
8. Talent on set
9. On-set participation

C. Post-Production

10. Coordination and management
11. Graphics, screenshots, and animation
12. Music
13. Editing
14. Delivery and distribution

Pre-Production

Project Concept, Goals, and Schedules

Every journey begins with a first step. When creating your video project, this first step usually involves a series of questions, especially if you decide to work with an online video production company. Everything from the type of video you envision, to your budget, to your desired goals for the video should be decided before the video concept is determined.

It is necessary during this phase to consider the current marketing messages that you are providing to your customers. The information on your marketing materials and in your purchase funnel can provide a beginning for this phase of the project. You may be reaching your customers via print, television, billboard, website, and pay-per-click ads. Decisions you make during pre-production will influence these other marketing activities and the marketing messages you are already projecting in the marketplace.

In most cases you don't start your pre-production from scratch. A lot of our customers use their website copy as a starting point. They will look at what they are trying to say on their website and transition that message into a message delivered via video. It is important at this step to integrate your current marketing goals into your video project. You are still targeting the same demographic and should use the same messaging as your other marketing activities.

During this initial pre-production process, you (if you intend to self-produce) or you and your production company will figure out the best steps for proceeding based on the information you have gathered. The goal here is to truly discover what your needs are and how best to move forward. Maybe you have an idea for a concept and need to brainstorm further with your team, or perhaps viewing video examples will help you figure out exactly what you want. Every stage of the process will need to be figured out in pre-production.

With a concept in hand, the next step is figuring out what resources will be needed for production. Does the shoot require on-screen talent? If so, is this on location or in a green screen studio? Is it voice-over talent only? If so, what will the visual component of the video be? Will there be animations or motion graphics? What type of crew will be needed to complete the project?

Once all of this is determined, the process of creating a schedule can begin. Although a typical shoot is only one day, the pre- and post-production phases may take days and even weeks to complete. The schedule established by you or your production company should take this into account. It should also outline your individual responsibilities. Are you creating the script? When is it due? Do you need to provide approval on a completed draft? Following the schedule and knowing what roles and responsibilities are yours will keep your project moving forward.

Scriptwriting/Storyboarding

Once the concept and direction of your video is figured out, you can begin to develop your script. You can do this in-house, hire an outside writer, or have the video production company assist you with this step. We recommend that our clients write a first draft of their video script. This isn't due to a lack of scripting knowledge on our part. It's actually more of a study in corporate identity. Our clients know their own company. Seeing how they perceive themselves on paper allows us to incorporate this information in future script drafts and visual images. Whether or not you hire a professional to write your script, consider taking the time to jot down a first draft to see how you would tell your company's story via video.

The most important part of the scripting process is retaining the focus on your concept for the video. Don't delve into any other information. This is the time to create a distinct and on-point message. Got something else to say? Create another video. And it's been said before, but I'll say it again: keep your script short, simple, and on subject. If your video allows for it, include a clear call to action for your viewers.

Scripting isn't just about the words on the page. It also has to do with the images that you want to represent your company on-screen. This will depend on the video you are creating. I typically work with a script template that delves into (1) the words the

Table 7.1 Innovate Media Sample Script Set Up

Client Name:	Video Title:
Delivery/Host URLs:	Link for "Click Me" URL:
Producer: John Cecil, 714–352–7200	Circle video walk -in position: left, right, static
Talent Needed:	Wardrobe description:
Script Version:	Spokesperson Size:
Date:	(For selections, see innovatemedia.com/size)
VIDEO	AUDIO
This space is reserved to detail the images or graphics you would like to accompany your on-screen or voice-over video talent. You only need to fill out this section if your video includes visuals. If your video includes the video spokesperson feature, you will not need this section of the script filled out. The length of this text box will increase as you prepare your image and graphic details for your viewers.	This section of the script template is reserved for your script, and the actual words your talent will read on or off camera. Font should be Courier New 12 point and paragraph line spacing set at 1.5. One full page of this template is roughly equal to 60 seconds of video footage. The length of this text box will increase as you prepare the words and text-based message for your customers.

Source: innovatemedia

talent will read and (2) the visuals that will be shown on-screen. Determining what you want to show on-screen before you actually film anything will not only save you time, but it will also save you money. One of the biggest time drains during post-production is figuring out what to show visually. If you don't know at this point, you'll be paying an editor or your production company to find a solution for you. So whether it's as simple as your logo or screenshots of your website, start thinking of the visual components of your script early.

A sample script has been included for your reference. One full page of content, using the setup information below, will roughly equal 60 seconds of video footage. The left side of the script outlines what images will be shown and when. The right side is for the script dialogue itself. Use the following word-processing settings for your margins, font, spacing, and paper position will help you organize your script and also provide an estimated length of your content:

- Top margin 0.43 inches
- Bottom margin 0.43 inches
- Left margin 0.42 inches
- Right margin 0.42 inches

- Select portrait orientation for your paper
- Select left as your gutter position
- Set your header and footer at 0.5 inches each
- Use 8.5 × 11 inch paper size
- Set line spacing at 1.5
- Use Courier New 12-point font

And if your video concept allows for storyboarding, this can really be a great way to visualize your ideas before they come alive on the screen. Storyboarding can be as simple as creating a few images to showcase your ideas. But it can also go as deep as hiring an animator to create a whole series of stills that can be utilized once production and post-production begin. Much will depend upon your budget and the project you hope to create.

Asset Gathering

Assets are the graphical elements that will be used as visuals for your video. I mentioned earlier that videos are often built backward, and asset gathering is one of the reasons for the reverse process. Although the actual placement of the visual components of your video will come during the post-production process, the sooner you gather these assets the better. Examples of assets are a company logo, visual elements taken from a website, graphics, screenshots of a user interface, and photos of a facility or a product. If you give your video producer a logo for your video, you want that logo to be filled with life on-screen, not just a still, flat image as it is on your brochure or stationery. In many cases an asset can be turned into a motion graphic to support the video's flow.

Not only will you know exactly what visuals will be shown on-screen, but the project as a whole will also be streamlined and on schedule. Having your assets available by the time production wraps up and editing begins is crucial for your production schedule and timeline. The sooner an editor has your assets and the filmed footage, the sooner he or she can get to work and provide you with a final video reel.

You'll want the images used in your video to be as high resolution as possible. So whether the images are of your logo, screenshots of your site, shots of your products, or stock footage, make sure that the quality of these assets is good. In terms of size, bigger is definitely better for production purposes.

Hiring Talent

Who is your target demographic? Who will they want to watch? Whether on-screen or voice-over talent, finding the right actor is key to having a believable presentation regarding your business or product. When working with a production company, they typically will help you find the right person for the job by conducting a talent casting based on the demographic you desire. You will then be given the top performers as options to choose from. Conducting a talent casting for your video, however, often does come with a higher price tag.

We help offset this cost for our clients by providing self-selection talent information. Via our website, clients can view a list of talent available for project shoots. This special page lists the video auditions of a wide range of talent. Many we have worked with, and others we aspire to work with. A wide selection of actors and actresses, representing all ages, shapes, ethnicities, and native languages, is available for clients to review. Our talent page also allows customers to preselect talent based on their needs without having to go through the cost of demonstrating in-person talent.

Hiring voice-over talent is a similar process to finding those who will appear on-screen, although it is often a less time consuming and costly endeavor. Services such as Voice123 allow production companies and individuals alike to post their jobs and open up this listing to professionals who fit their description. Voice-over talent then applies for the job by sending a demo reel or custom-made audition piece. You then choose the "winner" of your job, and they can send you the final take based on your specifications. Services like this make the process of finding talent simple. Contracts, rates, and the actual job are already posted, so any talent auditioning for your role already knows, and has agreed to, the terms listed.

One thing to always consider when hiring talent is the contract and payment system involved. If you are working with a production company, they are most likely hiring the talent on your behalf and handling all of the payments and contracts. However, you will want to verify if you are required to pay yearly residuals to the talent for continued use of their likeness or if the contract states use in perpetuity. Also realize that the usage of your video in terms of the contract with the talent is most likely "for Internet use only." Be conscious of what the terms include. By using your video in other mediums, such as television, you can violate the terms of your contract and may be liable for paying any damages to the talent.

If you're booking talent yourself, you'll really want to be up front with the usage and scale of your video. Unfortunately, it is still a major misconception that online-based projects are of the same caliber budgetwise as broadcast productions like TV commercials. Booking talent at the standard union rate for a commercial can quite easily be larger than the entire budget of an online video project. So before hiring anyone, be sure they understand you are creating a nonunion video project for Internet usage only. This way both you and the talent are on the same page.

Production Variables

These are some smaller things that may come into play with your shoot depending on the video you are creating. However, they still should be considered before production begins.

Wardrobe

If your project calls for on-screen talent, the clothing that the talent wears is of utmost importance. It's a powerful visual cue that sends a signal to your audience and shows them how you want to be perceived. So if you are looking for a corporate professional look, have your talent dress accordingly. Or if you can be more casual with your choices, have a look that is still appropriate. Other considerations are colors and patterns—not every choice works on-screen, especially if you are filming on a blue or green screen. If the talent you are hiring does not have the proper clothing, don't be afraid to ask them what their size is and purchase suitable attire for them.

Hair and Makeup

If you're going through the trouble of hiring talent or using your CEO as your on-screen personality, hire a reputable makeup artist. For a nominal fee, you and your talent can be reassured that they will look good on-screen. And if you're working with a production company, this is a service they should be providing.

Production

Shoot Day

Understand the elements that go into a shoot day. Days, weeks, and perhaps months of planning go into the orchestration of the day when your video footage is finally shot. If you are hiring a production company, much of this day is already mapped out for you. But if you are filming internally, or you or a colleague is going to be on camera, there are some things to think about. If the location is your office or any of your staff are the talent, make sure that the space and people being filmed are prepared. Clean up the office, have the space for filming figured out, and carve out a place for the crew.

Even if you aren't in front of the camera, shoot days can be stressful and tense. Shoot time flies quickly. There are many moving parts, and a flurry of activity is needed to keep things on schedule. But this is why you prepared so much during the pre-production stages. Stay focused on what you need to get done; don't waste time trying to get everything perfect if you don't have time, and don't try to do everything yourself. This is unfortunately how mistakes happen.

Equipment and Crew

If you're hiring a production company, this element of the shoot will be taken care of for you. They will be responsible for the equipment and crew that will be used during the production of your video footage. The equipment will be their own or rented, and the crew will either be their staff or freelancers.

If you are doing the video shoot yourself, you can rent the equipment and do the filming on your own or hire a few freelancers who can help make the process of filming go much smoother. Remember, your video project is a bigger endeavor than just pressing the record on a camcorder. This is a video representing your business, so you'll want to create something as professional as possible, within your budget. Hiring local pros to handle things like lighting and sound will most definitely give your project

Figure 7.1 Innovate Media Shoot Using The RED Camera

higher production values. But seeking out film students could also give you a crew with some working knowledge of what you need to do.

Talent on Set

If your project has on-screen talent, you've already gone through the process of hiring the right person based on your desired demographic and creating a contract. Or you have met with and prepared associates from your company who will be acting as on-screen talent. Here are some things to keep in mind during the production phase:

Prepare the Talent

Make sure the talent has the script in advance so they can prepare, even if a teleprompter is available. You'll also want to make sure that any staff to be on camera are comfortable with the script and have practiced with the teleprompter. If it is an interview format, make sure they have the talking points studied.

Give Direction

Make sure the talent has a clear direction for the performance they are to give. Is this a more corporate video where they need to act like a business professional? Are they supposed to evoke a caring and understanding persona because of the sensitivity of the subject matter? It may be obvious from the script they are to read, but be sure that the talent is clear on their performance.

On-Set Participation

It's not always necessary for you to be at the shoot if you have hired a production company. If you have done a good job in the pre-production process and have prepared the scripts and provided clear direction on the actor's dress, hair, and mannerisms, you should be fine with leaving the production in the hands of your hired crew.

On the other hand, depending on your product or service, you may need to be present at the shoot. For example, TV Ears, a major distributor for wireless television listening devices, has a very technical product. They create videos for their customers to explain product details and increase conversions. Because of the intricacies of the product they offer, a company representative needs to be at the studio or on location during the shoot. During the filming, it helps to have their person there to answer last-minute questions the talent may have, or to demonstrate additional workings of the device. When we put the shoot together, we always schedule it at a mutually convenient time to ensure that their representative will be present. It would be impossible for our crew to refer to the script and fully understand what to shoot. In this case it really helps to have the customer there to make sure we get the right shots.

Post-Production

Coordination and Management

Once the footage has been captured, the post-production process begins. Most likely if you work with a production company they will assign you to a production coordinator who will guide you through and manage this process for you. During this phase, your project will be given to an editor who will work on it according to the script and/or storyboard prepared in pre-production. Your assets will be incorporated along with the filmed footage. Based on the complexity of your video project and the project schedule, you will be given a first version of your video. You then will be able to respond with comments and feedback.

Graphics, Screenshots, and Animation

If you completed all the steps in pre-production, most of your visual assets are already gathered at this point. But holes do come up, and elements often need to be captured or created. This step was mentioned earlier in pre-production because of the time involved in gathering these assets as well as the importance it has on the overall look of your project. Without any visuals, your video is simply a voice-over or a talking head. This does not make for a very compelling video.

If you're working with a production company, the editor will most likely use some sort of motion graphics technique on your project. This is something that will definitely be determined by your budget, but it also is the reason why some videos are exciting and have movement, and don't just look like flat 2-D images. Even if it is just an interesting logo effect, the use of motion graphics can take your video from boring to stellar. If you're looking for true 3-D animation, the cost and complexity of this is obviously related to your budget and video concept. Look to your video production company for further guidance.

Music

Music can certainly make a major impact in your video project. It has the power to invoke emotions and feelings, just like the words your talent speaks or the visuals shown in your video. It is a very subtle but powerful effect. Since music is so subjective, we always recommend that our clients participate in music selection. We often have them give us a few descriptive words and a style of music they are looking for. From here, we provide a list of options for them to choose from. We often get our music selections from music sites like 5Alarm Music, which has a vast array of collections and libraries to choose from. Music on websites like these is typically provided on a "per-use" basis, and customers must pay a fee. The fee depends on how the music track will be used that one time. So if you want to use a music selection for more than one video, for example, during a multi-video series, you will pay for the same music each time it is used in each of the videos. It doesn't matter if it's one video or a hundred.

Simple Mobile pays for the same music track that runs through each of their four videos. The videos were produced for their trade show, and the music is part of their theme. Although it is the same music, Simple Mobile had to pay for it four times. There are also different music usage licenses available, and they have different price points, depending on the project and use. For Internet usage, 5Alarm bases their fees on how many views the project is estimated to receive.

Another music purchase method is known as royalty free. You pay one fee for the track and then you can use it multiple times without paying additional fees or royalties, as long as the use fits within the agreed license. You can also look for buyout privileges for your music purchase so that you won't have recurring fees. Like stock photography, once the item is yours, it's yours forever, and you can use it in as many videos as you like based on the terms of usage. However, the selection of music available from buyout sites is often more limited. But if you are working with a production company, they should be able to guide you in making the best decision for your project and budget.

Editing

This is where everything comes together for your project in post-production. All of your filmed footage, assets, music selections, and so forth are given to an editor who will work his or her magic to create the finished video. After selecting the best takes of your filmed script, the raw footage is "digitized" so that it can be worked on with editing programs like Final Cut Pro. A rough cut with the footage and audio in sync is then created to set up the proper time-line. With that, your visual assets are laid out in the script and the storyboard components are assembled together. The use of motion graphics, animation, music tracks, and sound effects help bring this all together into one cohesive video. Once all feedback has been given and the editing has been completed, the final sound mix and render of your video are produced during the mastering process.

Delivery and Distribution

When your final project is complete, it will most likely be given to you in a file that you can download from the Web, such as a .MOV or .MP4. Most online video production companies don't deliver hard copies of video projects unless you give them something such as a drive to place it on. You then have the option to deliver the video to your site from the options given in chapter 6.

Green Screen Production Model

Filming a video in front of a green screen offers you a ton of flexibility in the final video project you'd like to create. From a "talking head" video spokesperson to a video filled with motion graphics and animations, utilizing a green screen can provide a solid way to produce a video on any budget. Not familiar with this concept? We utilize this method in 90 percent of our video projects, as it gives us an amazing array of options to work with.

Our client Canon wanted a video of a woman in a park. The images were to include the active use of one of their cameras in an outside environment. Our green screen technique provided an opportunity for us to work with Canon on this project and ensured that the project would be within budget.

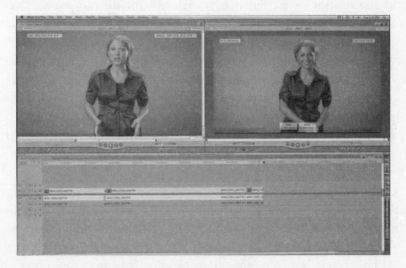

Figure 7.2   Woman in the Park Using Green Screen Technology (from green screen shoot)

We shot the actress in front of a green screen—in the studio. She was holding Canon's camera of choice while reading her scripted lines. Then one of our photographers took still shots and background shots in the park. The production crew did not go to the park, there were no film or entertainment permits or fees required from the local city government, and the sound technicians did not have to filter out waterfalls, birds chirping, or a jet overhead.

The result was a video of the actress actively using Canon's product in a park setting just like the client requested. The client paid less, and the project came in on budget. In the final video, viewers had no idea it was shot in front of a green screen.

This technique was born of necessity, as it made it possible to scale our production shoots and costs based on the demands of our clients. Instead of creating a set for each project, we simply had to film the talent in front of a green screen. The "space" the talent would inhabit was all developed in post-production.

An example of this model is Children's Hospital of Orange County (CHOC). Most of their videos are testimonial-based content. We film a doctor or a patient in an office or hospital setting. Sending a crew out and setting up the lights and camera every time CHOC needs a new testimonial would not be cost effective for them. We would need to charge them for the crew, and in many cases only one doctor is available on a certain day. To send out a crew to shoot one doctor does not make sense. Instead they send the doctor or patient to our studio during our green screen shoot days. We hold their time and shoot footage of whoever they need captured. We don't charge them for "lights, camera, action!" for the entire day, and we can shoot multiple people on that same day. Back at the studio, post-production begins, and we insert the appropriate office or hospital background into the film. With improvements in technology and camera equipment, the end user watching the video can't even tell it was not shot at the actual "location." The green screen technique has worked for this customer and they keep coming back.

Green or blue screen filming is the same method used in big-budget action thrillers like *The Avengers* or even in the daily weather report. The soundstage the actors work on is typically painted green, and the talent is filmed at this location. In post-production, the world these characters live in or the alien invaders they may pursue are all developed. The same thing applies for your green screen shoot. By filming in front of a single color like blue or green, the background can be "keyed out" and replaced with something else, perhaps from another video clip, a stock photo, or a background that fits into the color scheme of your website or logo. With the "setting" of the video in place, you can then add in whatever you like, such as motion graphics, text, your logo, product shots, B-roll footage, or what have you. The possibilities of what you'd like to create are limitless. And unlike shooting something on a set, you can change and update the elements of your video, such as graphics or backgrounds, as needed.

To get started with your own shoot, you'll need the space available for a green or blue screen. There are plenty of ready-made options from camera stores, or a local studio in your area may also have a green screen setup that you can rent. No matter what option you choose, you'll want the screen to be of a uniform color and shade to make the process of keying out the green as simple as possible. If it is a piece of fabric, be sure that it hangs as straight as possible with no visible wrinkles.

Whether you choose blue or green to work with as your screen, be sure that whoever you are filming works with your choice. So, if filming on a blue screen, your subject should not have blue eyes or be wearing blue clothing. The same thing applies with green screens. And something that may be helpful in case there are issues with the footage you have is thinking about what background colors your video may incorporate once in post-production. Choosing a screen similar to the colors used in the final video can minimize any errors that might occur when keying the edges, or shadows that might appear on your screen.

Another concern with your shoot is lighting. A green screen needs to be evenly illuminated and consistent so that it makes the background (which will be taken out in post-production) a single color to make the keying-out process as simple as possible. Multiple lights at different angles will most likely need to be used, so if you're renting, keep this in mind.

Not only do you have to create lighting that will properly showcase your screen, but you also have to light the subject properly so that they will have no shadows on them. Adjusting lights and using filters can help solve these problems.

Once filming has ended, your work is not done. Post-production is actually just beginning. You'll need to first remove the background screen color of your videos and replace it with the image you desire. Then comes the task of including any other assets you'd like in the video. You'll need the right software programs to be able to accomplish this effectively. Final Cut Pro or Adobe After Effects are two popular options for you to consider.

These are just some ideas about what it takes to produce a video. The pre-planning phase will always come first. In fact, that is the phase you're in now, if you will be creating your first video. Think about the decisions you'll need to make so that the project will be a success. Then move forward with confidence that you have the information necessary to help you make good decisions for your project and its impact on your business and your ROI.

In this chapter, you learned about the process of making a video step by step, the different choices you will be required to make as part of that process, and what options are available to ensure that your video engages your viewers and is professional. You also learned about the following:

- ☑ Production options available to help you create your video content because, as with delivery, you have choices that include self-production or professional producers;
- ☑ The roles and goals of all involved in the project;
- ☑ Animation, graphics, and music selection for your project;
- ☑ Why you may need to attend the on-set filming of your project;
- ☑ How the green screen technique can reduce your production costs;
- ☑ The pros and cons of hiring a production company or filming yourself;
- ☑ Tips for successful production;
- ☑ The process of a typical video production project from finish to start.

Now let's put it all together. The green screen technique has flexibility and is easy to use for a variety of projects. That's probably why it is one of our favorites. We have the flexibility to shoot multiple clients during one day without worrying about creating a specific set for each individual project. This allows us creative flexibility. If client A wants to incorporate product stills and motion graphics in their video and client B simply wants a video spokesperson, we can capture both types of videos on the same day since filming is essentially the same for each. Another benefit of this technique is the cost savings involved in scheduling multiple clients together on one shoot day. This is helpful to our clients because the costs can be spread out and scaled to fit their overall budget. We can also continue to rent high-quality RED cameras, have a professional crew, use stellar talent, and afford access to an actual working green screen soundstage.

A typical day under these conditions can set us back anywhere between $3,000 and $5,000 per shoot, depending on variables such as the amount of talent hired or the crew involved. For us to actually survive and make anything from our efforts, we do need to have at least $10,000–15,000 in booked business for the endeavor to make sense. However, having one client with a video project and this type of budget is not always realistic. This price point is far more than most clients have available or are willing to invest in video. But by scheduling multiple clients together on one day, it is possible to shoot a range of content for many different types of budgets. This is also good news for the "little guys" who may only have a budget of around $500 to create a video spokesperson. In this manner, the micro, mini, or solo business can still compete in the larger marketplace. At the same time, they can have quality video footage equal to that of the client who spends $15,000 on a hyperstylized motion graphic piece. What makes this method great is that all clients can receive a high-quality video production without having to pay the full cost of a single shoot date.

A price differentiator in online video is the quality and quantity of post-production work involved. If building a video is much like building a house, then the foundation may be the same, but the materials used to create the final product are what determine the price. For your kitchen floors, for example, you can have something low end like Formica or high end like travertine. You'll get a floor, but the finished quality of that floor is really up to you and your budget. The same goes for video. The more intense the graphics are, or the cooler your viewers think it is, the higher your price tag.

No matter what the budget, a lot of time and work are involved with each video project. You will be spending this time yourself if you decide to produce in-house. Hiring a production company will keep your time available and give you guidance throughout the project. We have mastered the art of online video production, but it has taken us some time to learn, and we've been at it since 2003. Much was trial and error. Hopefully you're reading and learning from our not-so-good experiences. New technologies and trends, especially for post-production, force us to evolve and learn more. So don't be frustrated if you do decide to take on the production of video content for yourself or your company. In time, you will learn what content and methods work best for your needs.

•

CHAPTER 8

Video SEO—The Science of Getting Seen

So you've produced a great video and have successfully delivered it onto your site. But who's exactly going to see it? Up until now, we've discussed video in relation to production and delivery. But just how can you make sure an audience sees your video? This is where the science of search plays a part in your video strategy in the form of video search engine optimization (SEO). Video SEO is one of the greatest opportunities available to businesses and marketers for developing an audience and driving traffic to their site.

According to a recent study by Forrester Research, videos with a properly submitted sitemap were 53 times more likely to generate a first-page Google ranking than traditional, text-based SEO techniques. In other words, video SEO is a powerful resource that you *must* incorporate into your total strategy. So what exactly is video SEO? Like traditional search engine optimization that uses text-based metadata via an XML sitemap to get your website or blog picked up by search engine "crawlers," video SEO also tries to get your video seen by consumer search engines. This information, in the form of a thumbnail, descriptive title, keywords, tags, and a URL, can then be submitted to search engines.

Video SEO differs from traditional SEO because video SEO offers a unique advantage to your search strategy. Search engines crawl through the Internet looking for content in different formats such as text, images, and videos. This content all appears as search results. When you have optimized your video sitemap, you increase your likelihood of being ranked higher. Why? These blended search results give a higher ranking to video content. This is why it is so important to have a clear and well-developed video SEO strategy; doing so can dramatically increase your search rankings and site traffic.

It's not just about new techniques versus old techniques. Video SEO needs to be thought of as a completely separate strategy from traditional text-based SEO. From this moment on, your video search strategy will be in addition to whatever your other discoverability efforts are. Unfortunately, the importance of video as a key SEO tool is not always fully realized. Companies are either (a) ignoring video SEO altogether by only submitting the pages on which videos reside and not the videos themselves, or (b) submitting their video assets to YouTube with the misunderstanding that this submission will generate SEO benefits for their own website. Both of these ideas could not be more wrong. Here you'll learn the following:

- ☑ What you need to do to create an effective video SEO strategy;
- ☑ The difference between posting versus hosting;
- ☑ The steps involved in implementing and submitting a video sitemap;
- ☑ The continued process and maintenance of video SEO.

Most importantly, the key takeaway should be that video SEO is an ongoing and important part of your marketing strategy. This isn't a single effort in which you submit a video sitemap once and you're done. You will continually need to be working on video SEO.

Going Viral

Viral videos are an anomaly. There are several examples of recent videos that were quietly uploaded to YouTube and became viral smashes that were viewed and shared by millions of viewers. Dream of producing your own video and feeling the wonder of it going viral. Trust me, it seldom happens. Customers usually ask, "How can I make my video go viral?" Getting a video to be viewed and shared by millions around the world is a feat that is going to take more than a properly submitted video sitemap. An abundance of creativity, an interesting subject, an emotional plea, complete absurdity—whatever the "it" factor may be is what keeps people watching, linking, and sharing. Video SEO may help get the word out about your content, but it certainly does not guarantee that your video will go viral. Instead of focusing on how to make your video the next Internet sensation, be realistic; use video SEO as a tool to get your video ranked at the top of the search engines. It's a much more obtainable goal.

Video Search

Think about how big search is, the millions of users each day who type a query into Google or Bing using just a few words to find information they need. They receive the information and then they take action. Let's say you are searching for something on Google. You'll receive multiple options on the subject you're searching for: everything from text, to images, to video, news, shopping, and more. What's now included, though, in these search results is video content in the form of a thumbnail image and a text description. Blended search results mean that both text and video content now appear. Words and pictures together are returned for each search you make, and it's becoming more common. If your strategy is executed properly, your optimized video content can provide huge results for your search marketing efforts. For example, Innovate Media submitted a sitemap for our video about our video spokesperson product. Utilizing the keywords "Video Spokesperson," we were able to achieve a first-page ranking in Google blended results and have seen a 30 percent increase in traffic to the page where the video resides. See the graphic below as an example.

Now that you know the basics of video SEO and search, we'll break the rest of this chapter out by strategy: video SEO using YouTube and other file sharing sites, and video SEO using an

Video spokespersons, Video spokesperson on your Website to ...
www.innovatemedia.com/video-spokespersons
Jul 16, 2011 - 29 sec
Video Spokespersons - Innovative Media is a leader in **Video Spokesperson** ... Contact us to learn how a ...

Figure 8.1   Video SEO Listing

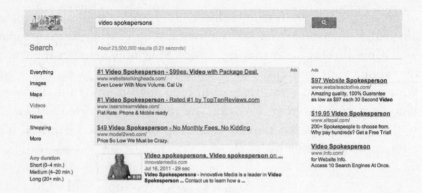

Figure 8.2 Google Blended Results Listing

online video platform (OVP). Most OVPs have video SEO tools inside them that can simplify the process of putting your sitemap into action. To have a completely foolproof SEO strategy, I recommend using both YouTube and an OVP to reap all the benefits video SEO has to offer.

YouTube's Place

By now you know that using YouTube alone as a way to deliver video directly onto your site is not a strategy I recommend. I have suggested utilizing an OVP for a multitude of reasons, including SEO benefits. However, YouTube does have an integral role in any well-developed video SEO strategy, which we'll delve into more when discussing posting versus hosting.

Unfortunately, though, the most common belief when using YouTube for video delivery is that by setting up a channel, uploading your content, and embedding the YouTube player on your site, you are somehow "done" with your video strategy and will automatically see SEO benefits. Unfortunately, this is not true. While videos uploaded to YouTube do appear in search results, the clicks off those listings will not go to your site but instead click through directly to YouTube. It doesn't matter where the embedded videos are originally posted, they will always click back directly to YouTube, giving them the SEO advantage.

Google owns YouTube. As a business, you should also be aware that content uploaded to YouTube technically becomes the property of Google. By contributing content to Google, you are also ceding all copyright to that work to them. This is not in your best interest if YouTube becomes your only strategy for video hosting and SEO. To increase the likelihood of driving traffic to your site as well as showing up in search results, you will not only want to use YouTube but also host your content directly on your site.

Posting vs. Hosting

There are basically two ways you can make your videos available online: "posting," which is the common method of uploading a video to public sharing sites such as YouTube, and "hosting," which is actually hosting your video content on your site either through an OVP or via your own means. Both efforts ensure a well-rounded SEO strategy. But let's now focus on the SEO advantages of posting. As the second-largest search engine, and by far the largest video sharing site, YouTube dominates this field. You want your videos on this site for pure reach and search potential. Other file sharing sites include Vimeo, which is great for higher-end content, and DailyMotion, which is used mainly in Europe and Asia. Vimeo's terms of service do prohibit the use of commercial content, so beware that as a business or marketer, you may be in violation and can be removed.

If there are other niche platforms in your industry that are popular, spend time using their services as well. If you do a lot of business internationally, why not upload content to DailyMotion for added SEO? But overall, you should spend most of your posting strategy focusing on the almighty YouTube.

Thumbnails

One element of video SEO that is completely different from traditional SEO is the need for a thumbnail. A thumbnail is an image, typically a still frame or screenshot of the video, that accompanies a text description in a video listing or search results. When creating a video sitemap, search engines do require that a thumbnail also be submitted. YouTube does have their own tool which allows you to choose a thumbnail from a few examples they gather from your content. Most OVPs also have similar tools that allow you to choose a thumbnail from a selection of available options. For example, figure 8.3 shows Oculu's own thumbnail tool. With

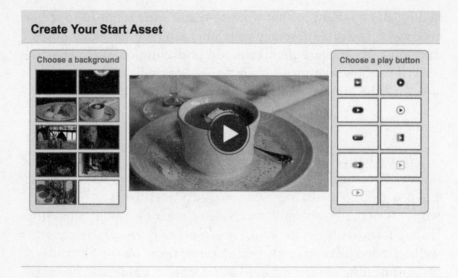

Figure 8.3 Thumbnail Example

Oculu, ten separate frames of the video appear for you to choose from as well as the option to choose your own play button.

Getting Started With YouTube

Since we've already established that YouTube is the largest and most important player in the "posting" field, let's focus on how to maximize your video SEO potential here. If you need to get started with a YouTube account, Google has helpful tips and tricks available regarding creating your YouTube channel or uploading a video here: http://support.google.com/youtube/?hl=en.

YouTube Metadata

To get found on YouTube and related video pages, you'll need to provide metadata in the form of clear, keyword-filled titles and text descriptions. Just like how you would add keywords, a title, and descriptions for a WordPress blog, you'll want to do the same for your posted YouTube video. Having a well-developed metadata strategy not only helps you in video search results but also helps your video appear in related video searches. Let's check out how to do metadata creation from a video example from our YoOculu YouTube channel located at http://www.youtube.com/yooculu.

Building a Title

What are people searching for? What will make them want to click on your video? Why should they watch? This is the time to be specific regarding what your video is about. It's not the time to be flowery or fluffy with your language choices—you can save that for the description if needed. Use the title space to really define and explain what your video is all about so it stands the chance of coming in on a relevant search.

Creating a Description

This space is your chance for a major SEO boost by creating a video description that is as keyword-centric as possible. YouTube gives you a ton of space to work with, 5,000 characters, so use this real estate to your full advantage. However, only the first 140 characters typically appear in search results, so take extra care to fill this section with your key phrases and search terms.

You'll also want to start this section with a link to your site, home page, or a specific landing page—basically wherever you want to direct traffic from the YouTube video page. This link needs to include the entire address, starting with the http or https of your site. That way YouTube will actually allow the link to be clickable so that viewers can use it. And if you don't include this information? Then you are going to lose possible traffic to your site because no one wants to copy and paste a link into their browser. They will abandon the video page without viewing your site if they cannot click on your link.

Remember the 5,000 character limit? It's more than enough space to explain your video with an extensive description. Or what about using a transcript of the video content itself? Whatever approach you take, be sure to fill this space with as many related keywords and key phrases as possible to increase your search rankings.

Figuring Out Tags

You've already figured out two parts of the metadata puzzle—a succinct title and a detailed description. What's left? Tags. YouTube gives you up to 500 characters to use when tagging. Depending upon the length of your keywords, you can expect to have room for 20–50 tags. For optimum results, you should use as many tags as you can within this character limit. Having more tags increases the odds that your video will be viewed. Like your title, try to be as specific as possible in your tags. Remember, all of this is based on searches your customers will be performing. What keywords will they use to find you? Don't be afraid to use the obvious if necessary, like tags based on your brand or industry.

Do you have a specific product? It may not be in your best interest to spend too much of your character limit on specific product names. Potential viewers, and therefore customers, most likely don't know your product by name, yet. So really think about what they may be searching for and make sure your tags are appropriate.

Helpful Hints

There are keywords that can get you blocked by YouTube for being spam. Words like "buy," "cheap," and "free" are the big offenders, so try not to use these words if possible. Take the time to make the first few words in your title and description make sense so that it tells the "story" of your video. This should make sense as a whole and entice viewers to watch. Invest the time to create concise and specific keywords and phrases that relate to your video and to the words viewers may search for. Think of your metadata as a hierarchy of information, with the title at the top and your description and tags at the base. The title definitely has the most power in search results.

YouTube Playlists

A playlist on YouTube is a really great way to feature multiple videos by topic or theme. It's also a convenient way for you to include related video content that may interest your viewers. But best of all, a playlist puts you in control of this additional content so that you can lead viewers to what you want them to watch. Figure 8.4 gives an example of Simple Mobile using playlists to their advantage on their branded YouTube channel.

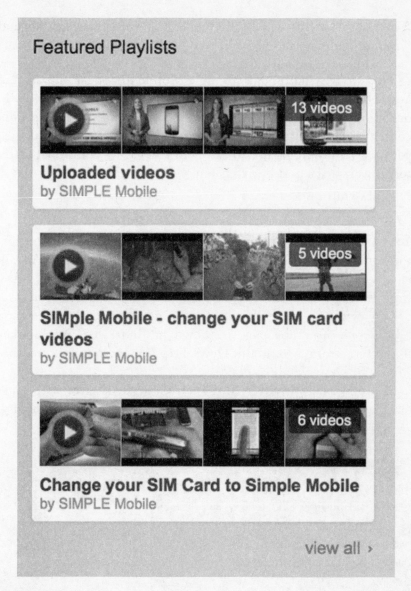

Figure 8.4 Simple Mobile

With three separate playlists displaying a mix of videos they've uploaded and user-generated content based on different themes like a video contest, they have successfully created the playlists using the following components:

A well-defined and logical theme for each playlist;
A clear, descriptive title;

A mix of self-produced and user-generated content is used, depending on the playlist.

This strategy has allowed Simple Mobile to appear on page 1 of YouTube results when searching for terms like "Simple Mobile" or "How to Change a SIM Card." Having multiple playlists and content from many sources, like Simple Mobile does, can only help your search rankings. It also can help you gather additional traffic to your playlists, and by extension, your content.

YouTube Pages

YouTube pages help link your video to related video content. Say someone likes your video enough to embed it on a page or add it as a link on a Facebook status update. These external "links" from social media and other sites are very important as they drive viewers to your video content. A great example of the capabilities of a YouTube page is shown in figure 8.5 in a marketing effort from Mountain Dew: http://www.youtube.com/user/ MountainDew?blend=1&ob=5.

Mountain Dew is advertising their Code Red flavor with musician Jay Electronica, with a page tailored around this campaign.

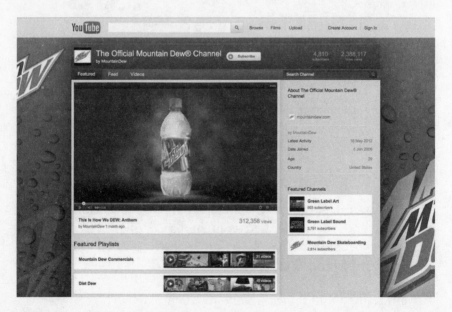

Figure 8.5 YouTube Mountain Dew Page

They have posted the recent campaign video as well as the related video content in the side bar. This dedicated channel is a surefire way to ensure that viewers are only seeing the content that you are putting up. The viewer can "like" the page on his Facebook account or easily post a tweet about it on Twitter. Your channel is a marketing tool to connect with the millions watching YouTube videos every day. As you gain more followers, they can view your recent history and easily comment on your channel. You can use this to build a large following and strengthen your business.

One important note is that the side videos on these pages get an incredible click-through rate, as it is typically related video content the viewer is interested in. Be sure that the other videos you place on your YouTube page are videos that will drive your marketing message or call to action.

YouTube and Duplicate Content

Posting duplicate content on YouTube can really be a negative with your SEO results. Google and YouTube don't want to see multiple versions of the same content being uploaded and indexed. If you have access to download other people's content and then publish it under your own channel, it's possible that this video, and even a related playlist, can be (1) filtered out of search results or (2) removed from YouTube completely. So if you are going to use other people's content on your channel, content that most likely is already on the creator's channel, do so wisely by adding the videos to a playlist rather than hosting them as your own. Other people's work should only be a "bonus" to what you upload and create.

Paid Techniques on YouTube

It's early in the world of paid video SEO strategies, but here is a look at the current paid techniques to help increase your results. If you're a frequent YouTube user and see the little yellow ads that you get on the first "promoted" results on some pages, especially when you search for something, these are really paid ads. The fact that this video appears is because that company or business is willing to pay a certain price for every click that people make.

Why would you want to pay for clicks on YouTube?

Figure 8.6   YouTube Paid Ads

1) Price. Currently click-through costs are very attractive. To give you an idea, at Innovate, we frequently buy the keyword "video marketing." On Google AdWords and Google's main search engine, we typically pay about three dollars per click. This is quite a bit of money for a click in comparison to YouTube, where the exact same keyword is less than 20 cents. And with YouTube clicks, you only pay when your video is actually watched; the viewer must watch a significant portion of the video for you to pay. If the viewer clicks and only a few seconds play, you do not pay.

2) YouTube Search. Your video will automatically appear on searches that relate to your keywords or phrases.

3) Related Videos. Your ad can appear on related video searches, targeting the audience that watches videos related to your keywords or tags. People watching this related content are already interested in the topic you present in your video, which makes them much more likely to watch your ad.

4) Google's Search Engine. By having ads on YouTube, your ad can also show up within Google's main page via video results. It's the same ad from YouTube, at the same cost, but it appears as an ad from a related search result on Google. Bottom line: it has the power to reach more people on Google than just on YouTube.

5) Rewards. Google rewards successful videos and channels. Basically, the more views you receive, the more prominently you'll appear on a search and related video content. Buying

ads is one known way of driving traffic to your YouTube videos. This doesn't mean that you're automatically placed in organic search results because you have bought ads. But if buying ads can help drive traffic to your video or channel, creating a wider audience, it is more likely YouTube will reward you through better placement in search results.

Hosting—Onsite Video SEO

Now that we've discussed posting your video on public platforms like YouTube for SEO benefits, it's time to talk about hosting the video on your site. As we've mentioned before, you can do this yourself or utilize an online video platform (OVP). To limit headaches and worry, the best option is to go with a reliable OVP who offers features like video SEO. Not only will they make video delivery to your site simple, but they will also most likely provide you with analytics and other features to help with your online video marketing efforts. Working with a professional hosting provider also ensures that your viewers receive a quality viewing experience with no buffering or skipping. Plus, you'll have tech support in case something goes wrong. And things may definitely go wrong. But most of all, the OVP you work with will most likely offer their own video SEO tool to make sure your video gets seen.

Video SEO Tools—Video Sitemaps

Just as you can index your website to be found by search engine "crawlers" via the use of keywords, tags, and other metadata, you can also do so for your video. Using a video sitemap tool, provided as a feature with many OVPs, is the easiest way to accomplish this. A video sitemap, which is an XML sitemap file, is a way to tell Google and other search engines that you have video content available on your site. Unfortunately, search engines cannot identify each video you post directly on your site. This is due to the fact that the number of video players and video hosting services is overwhelming; search engines just can't keep up. So it's your responsibility to tell them about your videos with a video sitemap. Your video sitemap will include all of the same metadata information we discussed with YouTube. You'll have a title, description, and tags, plus a URL, that all need to be thought about in terms of your video subject, audience, and keywords.

How Do I Know Google Sees My Videos?

The best way for Google and other search engines to "see" your videos is for you to create a video sitemap for your content. If you haven't done this, there's no way your videos are providing optimum SEO benefits. Once you have a sitemap created, you can find out if Google is picking up your video by creating a video search. This helps to ensure that your sitemap was properly submitted. Here's how to do it.

Go to Google video search and type into the search box "site:" and your URL/domain name (example: "site:innovatemedia.com"). You'll immediately be shown if Google sees the videos on your website as blended results. Click on the video search tab as well to see all of your videos that are being picked up by Google. If you find nothing, it means Google doesn't see the videos on your page. Either you have not created a sitemap, or it has not been properly submitted.

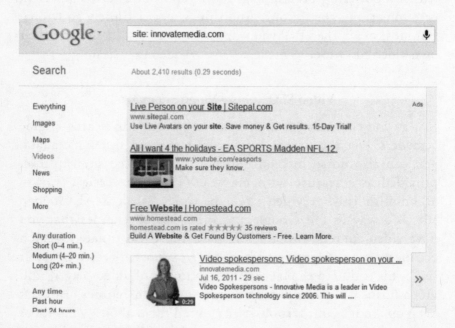

Figure 8.7 Google Listing Example

Creating a Video Sitemap on an OVP

Using an OVP to create your sitemap reduces the time and work involved in creating, hosting, and submitting the final product. Although there are many OVPs that offer a video SEO tool, the basic structure of creating the sitemap is the same:

1) Create the sitemap.
2) Add it to the "root" folder of your website.
3) Submit to Google via webmaster tool.
4) Check back often to ensure the sitemap is still working properly.

One of our competitors in the OVP space is Wistia, and they do a great job with their video sitemap submission tool. Their user interface is very simple, straightforward, and easy to use. Other sitemap tools from other OVPs, including Oculu, will be similar to Wistia's submission process, which is detailed below. The images and direction for their sitemap submission tool are taken directly from their site.

Setup

Getting started with video SEO on Wistia, like every other OVP, does require some setup. The first thing you need to do is authorize Wistia to host your video sitemap and reference pages on your site. This is done through a robots.txt file on your web server. The robots.txt is a file (almost) every website has that helps search engines know what content they can and can't index. The robots.txt also has the ability to inform and authorize sitemaps for your website. To get started, choose "video SEO" under the Account tab from any page in your Wistia account.

Next, you'll see the screen in figure 8.8 with instructions.

Now simply follow steps 1–3:

1. Copy and paste the line and add it to the end of your robots.txt file.
2. Type the URL of your robots.txt file.
3. Click the "Verify your robots.txt" button.

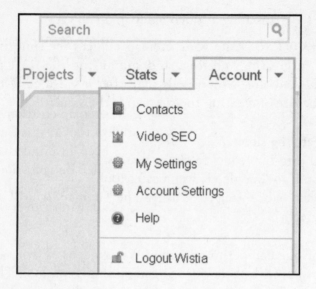

Figure 8.8 Wistia Site Map Example 1

Figure 8.9 Wistia Site Map Example 2

The last step helps verify that the information you have input is correct and viewable by Google and other search engines. Once you have completed these steps, you're ready to be found by search engines. What's left is to create individual sitemaps for your video content.

Sitemap Creation

The purpose of your robot.txt file is to allow search crawlers to find the video information on your site. Now you need to optimize each video's information with a sitemap in order to be found. Once this sitemap is created and submitted, it will automatically be picked up and indexed by Google. The sitemap creation process on Wistia is easy. However, their video SEO tool at this time only works with HTML embedded videos, so keep in mind that their tool only works if you have an embedded video on your site. Next, head to your video page within your Wistia account. You'll see the Media Actions menu as shown in figure 8.10. Mouse over this and select "Add to SEO Sitemap."

A dialog box should now appear so that you can enter the relevant information about your video, similar to what you've done for YouTube-hosted content.

Enter your title, a description, the URL the video resides at, and tags. When you are done, click on the "Add Video to Sitemap" button. Your sitemap is then automatically updated and sent to Google for indexing.

Figure 8.10 Wistia Site Map Example 3

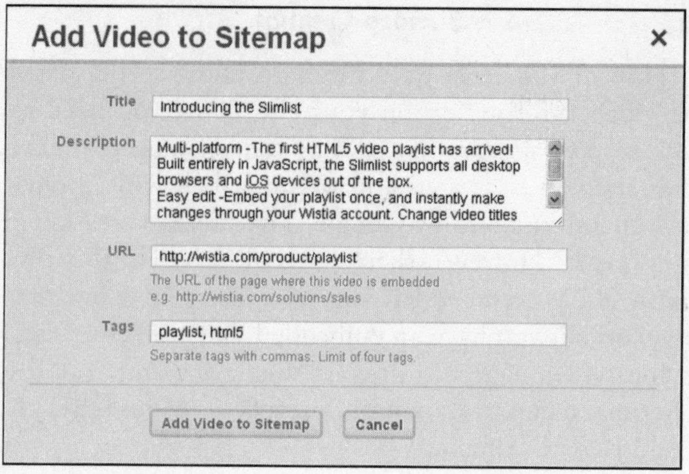

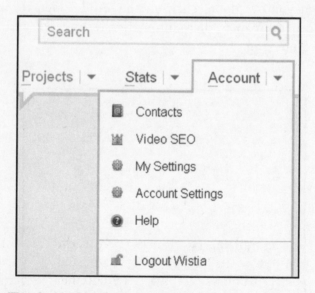

Figure 8.11 Wistia Site Map Example 4

Figure 8.12 Wistia Site Map Example 5

Managing Your Sitemaps

After creating and enabling your video sitemaps, you'll want to continually maintain and manage them. With Wistia, you can do all of this within the video SEO dashboard. Mouse over the

Account tab on any Wistia page and select "video SEO" to be taken to this dashboard. From here you can see all videos that are part of the sitemap, edit any of the sitemap information or video entries, and remove any unnecessary content.

A Few Pointers

Since video search is still in its infancy and is a dramatically changing process, using an OVP video SEO tool can help you simplify this task. But there are some things to keep in mind. You will want to do or know the following when using an OVP:

- Index both your video permalink pages and the videos themselves.
- Make sure that links point back to your site so you reap the SEO benefits, not your OVP.
- What search engines will your results show up in from your submitted video sitemap?
- Are there any analytics that can show the power of your SEO efforts and ROI?

YouTube vs. Your Site: An Epic Battle of Organic Search Results

I've recommended both "posting" and "hosting" your video content for maximum SEO benefits. But let's state the obvious: Google wants, and will list content from their entities higher in a video search than the content you have on your site. They want to drive that traffic, and any potential advertising profit, to YouTube. Even if you have done everything correctly with your site-hosted videos, like creating a video sitemap, using detailed and relevant metadata, and properly submitting this information to the search engines, a video search can result in your YouTube-posted video coming up first. Hopefully I don't sound schizophrenic here, because in past chapters I spoke against selecting YouTube as a delivery service for online videos. But for video SEO, it could be a good choice to include YouTube video placement to *complement* the videos already running on your own website. So instead of trying to beat Google at their own game, why not join them? Invest a lot of your time perfecting your YouTube channel and optimizing the metadata. If people are going to search on your keywords, at least you'll have done everything you can for your YouTube channel videos to appear on page 1 rankings. Then, as your "B" team, have the same optimized video content on your site to further help your SEO results.

Don't Forget about Traditional SEO

With all of this talk of video SEO to maximize search results and traffic, you don't want to forget about traditional SEO. When placing a video on your page, make sure to include lots of relevant text regarding your video directly on the page where the video resides. This could be a short recap of the video using keywords, or if it's a tutorial or how-to video, why not use a transcript as your text? This way you'll have an optimized sitemap related to your video as well as text from the page.

Another point to reinforce is that not only do you want to submit the sitemap for your video to search engines, but you also want to submit a permalink sitemap from the page the video resides on. Both of these should be similar to, and in fact mirror, one another. More often than not this trick gets overlooked, but it helps you achieve the highest page ranking possible.

On-Your-Own Video Hosting

So you're venturing into hosting and video SEO without an OVP? No problem. Although using an OVP makes the process of submitting a video sitemap much easier, you can still do this by submitting your own sitemap to search engines. Before you do this, you may need to contact each search engine for specific guidelines on submitting a video sitemap. As video SEO is ever changing, the information published on a particular site may be outdated. And unfortunately this is not a one-size-fits-all solution; each search engine is unique in the way they do things. As of this writing, Google has a great support section with information on their guidelines for video sitemap submission to help you create increased views of your video: http://support.google.com/webmasters/bin/answer.py?hl=en&answer=80472.

This chapter was packed with information about the following:

☑ What you need to do to create an effective video SEO strategy;
☑ Posting versus hosting;

☑ How to implement and submit a video sitemap;
☑ What you need to continue your video SEO strategy.

Overall, video SEO is the science to get your video, and by extension your company, seen without relying on a viral video. With the right keywords, a well-developed sitemap, and a strategy of both posting and hosting, you will have an optimized SEO plan in place that is sure to get results.

CHAPTER 9

Make Your Videos Social

S o far we've covered online video through the process of production to delivery to video search optimization. Even with a well-produced video, a targeted and to-the-point message, and an optimized SEO plan, there is still another method you can use to ensure viewers find you via video. But not viral video. Most Internet users are utilizing social media one way or another, and this trend is giving the masses a clear and distinct voice like no other medium has done before. Not only can users update friends and family with photos of their recent vacation, but individuals can go directly to product and service websites to give the "world" their feedback, be it positive or negative. Social media has made communication between customers and companies completely direct. There is no "middle man," and your customers can directly confront you about problems they may be having or about how awesome they think your product is. And this filter-free communication has the potential to make a real impact on your marketing efforts, especially when it comes to the ability to share your videos. Social marketing between businesses and consumers is easy; business-to-business (B2B) marketers may find it challenging. Video will help you overcome some of the difficulties of B2B marketing to your customers. In this chapter, you'll learn the following:

☑ Why incorporating video into your social media campaigns is important;
☑ Best practices for social and mobile video use;
☑ How video is utilized within the major social networks;

☑ A real working example of how two Fortune 500 companies used the power of video and social media to reach an entirely new demographic.

Search vs. Social

Search has always been a proven method of discovering the information you need when you need it. But what happens when this information comes from your social sphere—your friends, coworkers, business associates, and other trusted suppliers of content like articles, music, and videos that you may also want to peruse and enjoy? This is where social media comes into play, and it has the power to get your video, and your business, seen. Social networking has the ability to increase visibility in the way people utilize the information they need. Who better to enlist than your social and professional circles?

But social media isn't just about Facebook and Twitter. Think of it as an entire delivery platform, a content distribution mechanism like television, where you are literally broadcasting your message, via video, to an entire community. YouTube's tagline isn't "Broadcast Yourself" for nothing; social media can take your video messaging and direct it at engaged and targeted traffic with the click of a mouse. So from this moment on, your video isn't just a marketing message; it's quite literally social media itself.

And just like the social media marketing plans you have for your company, *video should be an integral part of this strategy.* So whether through a Facebook update on your business page, a link in a tweet, or a video FAQ shared on LinkedIn, video needs to be a part of your social media efforts.

In this chapter, we won't go into the foundations of social media, what it is, or how to use a specific platform. We will assume that you and your business already understand social media marketing. We're not going to tell you how to gather more likes, gain more followers, or increase your comments. But what you will learn and understand is the importance social media has on your videos and how your business can reap the benefits of social sharing.

The Power of Sharing

The biggest advantage, and possibly disadvantage, with social media and video is the power of users having a choice not only in the content they want to view but also in what they want to share within their networks. How does your video fit in? By providing a way for a viewer to engage with your content, and by extension, your brand. And not only is it possible for your video to be viewed by a user, but it is also able to be viewed by that person's connections, and their connections, and their connections. The possibilities are rather endless in getting your message into the marketplace.

But social media also gives your company a choice. It gives you the option to directly communicate the goals and objectives of your business, to answer any questions or resolve any problems, and to basically be involved in a conversation with your customers or potential acquisitions. It's a powerful tool, and using videos with it can only help you further promote your product, service, or brand.

Making Your Video Friendly to the Masses

Before we discuss each social network specifically and how they work with video, here are some key ways you can make your videos more likely to be shared and distributed among social viewers:

B2C versus B2B

As a marketer, promoting a business socially can create a challenge no matter who you are targeting. But the results are different depending on whether you're reaching a B2C or a B2B audience. Business to consumer social strategies can offer a lot more possibilities in reach because so many social users are your potential customers. On the other hand, reaching out to other businesses presents an entirely different, and much more difficult, approach; your target audience is using social media to reach their target audience too. Using video can improve your social media campaigns, so think of what type of videos would be most helpful for sharing. If you're a B2B company, is it video tutorials on how to use your service better? And don't forget the people behind the businesses you want to reach. Using social networks like LinkedIn can help you target these employees.

(Your Content Is) KING OF THE WORLD!

You're a business, but that doesn't mean your videos have to necessarily be boring, especially if you are using them for social media. Your videos are most likely based on marketing who you are as a company, answering a question or concern viewers might have, or providing information on a topic relevant to your vertical. You are a marketer and you always want to talk to your verticals properly. Your verticals, as I see them, are your customers and prospective customers. "Vertical marketing" usually refers to an industry in which very similar products or services are marketed using very similar methods. Examples would be financial services, retail, and transportation. If your market is sailors, you could go very wide and offer all manner of sailing-related things a sailor might be interested in. If you go deep (vertical), you may just focus on being the best yacht supplier and the top go-to resource in that small area of yachts rather than all sailing equipment and supplies. Keep in mind that the goal of utilizing social media is to get people to actually watch and, more importantly, share your videos. So make videos that will interest them, not ones that just cover the information that is already included in the About Us section on your site. Always be concerned with your viewer and who will be watching.

Thumbnail

If you're sharing a link to a video on a site such as Facebook, be sure to have an intriguing image on display. Thumbnails were discussed in the last chapter in regard to creating a video sitemap, and the same rules apply here. Choose an image that accurately reflects the video content. And if your video includes talent, be sure to select an image featuring him or her so a user is more inclined to watch.

Sharing Is Caring

If you want your video to be seen and shared, then make it easy for your viewers to do so. Many OVPs offer sharing buttons within the video players so viewers can automatically share a video with their social networks with just a click when they've seen your video on a blog or on your site. With Oculu's sharing feature, you can actually create a linked page where your video will reside and you can directly share across a range of social networking sites. The link automatically sends viewers to the custom-designed page where your video will play. One of several services that easily allow you to incorporate social media sharing buttons is Share This. Their plug-ins allow you to add their service to a wide array of platforms, such as WordPress, for easy sharing by your viewers and customers. Find them at http://sharethis.com.

Mobile

To go one step further with the idea of making your videos as accessible as possible to your audience and their networks, think about the devices they may be using when engaging with your content. Mobile devices such as smart phones and tablets are being utilized by more and more people, and their web experience is completely different from someone using a desktop or laptop. With a mobile user, you have a much more engaged and, frankly, captive audience than someone who is working from a computer with a large monitor and multiple tabs open. You'll want to make the process of allowing these viewers to share your videos as easy as possible. Utilize social sharing buttons so they can get your message out to their networks. You can do this by creating a mobile version of your site so that the pertinent information you'd like a mobile user to see (e.g., your video) is easily displayed for them. Having a mobile version of your site puts the odds in your favor that a user will stick around to discover the content you have to offer. No one on a smart phone or tablet wants to attempt to access a clunky site that is not optimized for mobile viewing. If your site and videos are not able to be viewed properly on these devices, you're going to be missing out on sharing opportunities with your customers and leads.

Going Viral

Previously we discussed how video SEO can help your video be discovered but not "go viral." Social media is much the same way. Although the power of social media is certainly the driving force of Internet videos getting millions of views, the content of these videos is what makes them so shareable. Let's take Kony 2012 as an example. Released by the nonprofit Invisible Children in March 2012, the video amassed over 32,000,000 views in its first week alone. This prolific viewing was undoubtedly motivated by the human interest story and high emotional stakes represented in the video. So unless you have the content to entertain or captivate an audience of millions, your video most likely will not be going viral anytime soon.

Social Media Networks

Now that you know the reasons why your videos should be utilized in your social media efforts, let's discuss the major networks involved.

Facebook

With a member base almost as large as the entire population of North America, Facebook is the largest social media network. With millions of video views each month, it's also conveniently the third-biggest site for watching videos in the United States. So if your company isn't utilizing this *free* advertising and sharing space, it's a must. Facebook really advocates the use of videos on both personal and business pages. With the new timeline layout, these videos can be placed in the video section where all of your uploaded content can be stored. Take a look at this example from Simple Mobile's Facebook page.

Figure 9.1   Simple Mobile's Facebook Page

By clicking on the video section of their page, you are directly taken to all of their video content. And by simply clicking on a video, a viewer can not only watch the content, but "like", comment, and most importantly share it with their friends. When you upload a video or post a URL as part of a status update, it gets posted to your "wall" and then distributed onto the news feeds of your followers. If your followers engage with the video, such as by liking it or sharing it onto their wall, this then gets distributed to their friends' news feeds, and so on. And with the average Facebook user having around 130 friends, you can see how your content has the ability to quickly be viewed by a wide array of people.

Facebook provides an incredible vehicle to get your video viewed by more and more people. As we have discussed in this book, the more video views, the more conversions you will have for your business. With your video being shown as something viewed and shared by a "friend," it becomes more likely that one of these viewers will watch and continue the sharing process. Why? Because a "friend" suggesting a video gives the perception that this content is valuable, relatable, and more worthwhile to click, watch, and share again. Another important thing to think about is the fact that many OVPs, like Brightcove, have video plug-ins that allow viewers to directly watch your video within the news feed or your post. Viewers will not have to leave Facebook and interrupt the social sharing process to enjoy your content.

Twitter

Never underestimate the power of 140 characters. Twitter is a great way to get traffic to your videos from a very targeted and deliberate audience. Instead of showing an actual video through the platform, as you can do on Facebook or YouTube, with Twitter you are actually posting a link that can send the viewer to a URL where your video is available. So whether it's your site, a blog, a custom landing page, a YouTube channel, a Facebook status update, or what have you, there's a lot of power that you have as a business to drive traffic to a very specific video or site.

Because you cannot post a thumbnail or video on Twitter, only a link, it's really recommended that you use a URL shortening tool like bit.ly or TinyURL to maximize all of your available space. Not only does this give you more room for killer copy to get people to click and share, but it also gives you the ability to receive valuable feedback, such as how many clicks you receive from each tweet. With this data you can really gauge what your audience responds to and what works and doesn't work well for your business.

But quite possibly the most intriguing aspect of Twitter, especially for businesses, is the fact that you can directly communicate with any user, whether they follow you or not, by incorporating their @ name in your tweet. You can speak directly with customers and potential ones alike! Perhaps someone complains about your product or service via a tweet. How amazing would it be to directly respond to their complaint with a video? Or what if someone had a problem or inquiry? You could immediately tweet them a video tutorial or FAQ that gave them the right answer. Top-notch customer service plus a way to share valuable information about your business equals a complete win. But let's not forget about the sharing aspects of Twitter. Users can "retweet" anything you post, and their followers will receive it. And, as mentioned in the above Facebook example, if users retweet your content, and their followers retweet it to their followers, and so on, the chains of people engaging with your videos become almost endless. The more retweets, the more video plays.

YouTube

In the last chapter, we discussed YouTube in regard to SEO benefits. But something not to forget is that YouTube is essentially a social media network, a community of people banded together by the power of video. You can use this power to your advantage. By simply having your videos optimized on your own YouTube channel, you are gathering added awareness and SEO benefits on the second-largest search engine out there. Plus, you have essentially covered your bases in regard to social media. But incorporating the community behind this platform can also be beneficial. From having subscribers to your channel to users commenting on your videos, you can not only reach users with your content, but you can also get valuable feedback directly from the source.

The Other Guys

If you're using social media, you have to utilize the aforementioned Big 3 to really be in the conversation. But there are other players in the game that might also be beneficial to your efforts.

Google+

Google's play at social media isn't looking to be a formidable opponent to Facebook or Twitter, yet. But what it does have in its favor is the power of the world's largest search engine and their recent "social search" development. If a user is logged into Google and completing a search, they can choose to have "personal results" show up. These results stem from connections the user has on Google+. For example, while writing this paragraph, I was logged into Google and then typed the phrase "online video." The personal results I received are shown in figure 9.2. The very first image on the page is a thumbnail for a video example that was posted on Oculu's account. Other articles and results also appear that are related to the query. With social media becoming closer to a search platform, having a well-managed Google+ page with lots of video content could be an excellent way to guarantee dominance in search engine results. The jury is still out on search versus social.

Figure 9.2   Sample Search Results Including Google Plus and Video Thumbnails

But if the above example is any proof of where Google+ is going, you can see how social video integrated with search is a total win.

LinkedIn

This for-business social network also lets you post videos. LinkedIn is a great tool to find more information on specific people, but more importantly, it also lets users research and explore what specific companies are all about. By using the SlideShare tool offered by LinkedIn and videos from your YouTube account, you can "share" your video content with colleagues, customers, and leads via LinkedIn. This is a great way to share important information not only about your business, but also about topics relevant to your industry. Perhaps you have a video that demonstrates a particular feature of your product or a filmed discussion or event that you'd like others to see. It's possible to let those you are connected to or who are in search of more information about your business see your video content.

Pinterest

The new kid on the block in social media allows users to "pin" images, and now videos, from anywhere on the Web to their virtual

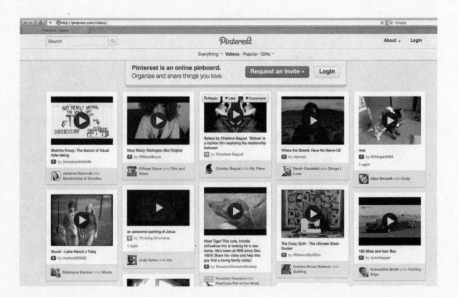

Figure 9.3 Pinterest Page Including Video Results

pinboards. So if a user finds something interesting on your site, like a video, they can easily capture it and place it onto a themed board.

Or they can grab this same content from boards your company creates. Just like how you can "share" on Facebook or "retweet" on Twitter, you can "repin" interesting content on Pinterest. Once again, the sharing possibilities are endless. Another compelling feature is that viewing a "pinboard" allows a user to post the content to their Twitter account or directly embed it into a blog post. So if your video is being shared on Pinterest, it can not only be discovered there, but also be readily shared to other networks as well.

Bringing It All Together

Hopefully, you now understand the value of incorporating your video content into your social media efforts. Let's now review a successful strategy implemented by two Fortune 500 companies. This is a good example of two so-called boring B2B marketing companies using social video. In the summer of 2011, Toshiba and Intel teamed up to create a social media and viral video campaign to further establish their brands with a very specific audience target— the young, hip, and social-media literate. Although both brands are huge players in technology, they weren't reaching the tech-savvy youth demo they desired. So they hired a talented young actress, locked her in a room with a laptop, and had a filmmaker known for making psychological thrillers film the entire thing.

Well, maybe it wasn't exactly like that.

Pairing the director of *Disturbia* with Emmy Rossum, the talent from the Showtime dramedy *Shameless*, Toshiba and Intel ventured to create a social film. The premise? Rossum plays Christina, a young woman trapped in an unknown location whose only link to the outside world is a Toshiba laptop with an Intel processor and an Internet connection. Not knowing where she is or by whom she was captured, Christina's only hope for escape is through her social media connections.

The trailer debuted on July 7, 2011, setting up the premise as well as a plea for video content. Viewers were instructed to submit video auditions if they would like to win a role featured in the final film. As if that weren't enough, viewers were also able to directly communicate with "Christina" beginning July 25 via Facebook, Twitter, and YouTube. Viewers submitted comments and messages that featured information on where Christina might be located or escape plans she might use to free herself. The multi-episode campaign actually utilized many of the user suggestions received from Twitter and Facebook to help build the story, giving followers an integral say in the plot, like a twenty-first-century "Choose Your Own Adventure" story.

The emotional ploy of aiding Christina as well as the fact that users could actually become a part of the story ultimately made this video series a victory for both brands. In just 11 days, the campaign attracted 10 million video views, 130,000 tweets, 4 million Facebook messages and posts, and hundreds of press stories. But the real value was being perceived as edgy and cool by an entirely new generation of potential customers through the power of a completely unique social video campaign.

Although this example of branded entertainment is on a much larger scale than most companies' budgets allow, it does show the real power that both video and social media can have on a company, its brand identity, and overcoming the challenges of social B2B marketing. Like it or not, social media has given a real voice to literally everyone who participates in it. These users are not only using this newfound voice to communicate with friends and colleagues; they are also speaking about and to brands. The conversation is happening with or without your business. So why wouldn't you want to be a part of it?

Social media is powerful and provides another tool for you to use in your video marketing efforts. It has the ability to really spread the word about your business, not only to your customers and followers, but to a whole new set of users you most likely would not have been able to target without it.

In this chapter, you've learned the following:

- ☑ Incorporating video with social media is important;
- ☑ Best practices for social and mobile video use;
- ☑ How video is utilized within the major social networks;
- ☑ A real working example of how two Fortune 500 companies used the power of video and social media to reach an entirely new demographic.

You already know that video increases engagement and conversions when included on your site, but think of the possibilities when your content is shared across a multitude of social platforms. Your reach is now endless. As a marketer, you have new challenges for using social media platforms as part of your overall efforts. But now, as a video expert, make sure you include your videos when you go social with your business.

CHAPTER 10

Taking Your Video to the Bank

People love good stories, and video images tell stories better than simple text and graphics. Your customers are learning more while they are engaged and attentive, whether they are informational or educational messages. Your video, when created and delivered as recommended, has the power to engage your viewers and prompt a response. The content you create for your website will also increase the time your customers stay on your Web page, and what they buy—while feeding their desire to trust you. Compelling video content properly deployed will communicate your brand, educate, inform, entertain, and dazzle your website visitors. The job of the content you create must represent your company and help your viewers feel comfortable. Comfortable viewers become customers.

Keep your options in mind and make choices with your customers in mind, not your bottom line. Remember to include video content in each of your marketing efforts for the best increase in your revenue because your customers' lives involve video. Keeping these ten closing thoughts as the center of your focus and connecting them to your marketing efforts will boost your ROI. Using these ten items during your video marketing will help you get more revenue from your efforts:

1. Online video will increase your conversions when you follow the eight golden rules for production success and make delivery and production your priorities.

2. Each day of your life includes video. Analyze your opportunities to connect with your customers via video to enhance your sales because their lives include video too.

3. Increase views and decrease viewer abandonment by keeping your viewers engaged.

4. Video must be included as a priority in both your marketing plan and your purchase funnel.

5. Video will provide a direct return on your investment that reflects the quality and professionalism of your production and delivery choices.

6. Production begins with the pre-planning phase.

7. Video is a profit center for your company, not an expenditure. Your video project can pay for itself with your increased ROI. Whatever you spend on your videos can be returned in sales, so decide on your delivery and create professional content.

8. Production and delivery are the yin and yang of online video—you need to master both as part of your video marketing strategy.

9. Creating your plan for delivering your content to viewers before you begin production will make your project a total success. Format choices and free/fee platform decisions will directly affect the production of your content.

10. Viral videos are an anomaly. Roll up your sleeves and get your videos viewed often by strategically executing both video SEO and social video initiatives.

It is time for you to take your first step in video marketing or to enhance the video content you currently produce. Your video story does not end with this book. You are beginning a new chapter in your marketing efforts and developing new streams of revenue. Using this information will help ensure that your video ultimately creates the highest return on investment possible that can come from converting your prospects into paying customers.

APPENDIX

Guide to Video Delivery Services

1. Brightcove, Boston, MA 888.882.1880 www.brightcove.com

Brightcove is the 100-pound gorilla in the OVP space, and I mean that in a positive way. Their technology is amazing but probably overkill for most marketers since they are a little more expensive. They have on-demand platform use available and reach more than 100 million Internet users every month. The OVP can support social media sites and streams video to mobile devices smoothly.

2. Kaltura, New York, NY 800.871.5224 www.kaltura.com

Kaltura is part of the "Big 3" (Brightcove, Kaltura, and Ooyala), and they really tout their open-source platform where large companies with tech teams can integrate their own system. A sampling of their clients includes media, entertainment companies, educational institutions, and service providers. The features are easy to use. Kaltura provides several levels of service, maintenance, and professional development. Their products make syndication, engagement, analysis, and monetization seamless.

3. Oculu, Costa Mesa, CA 888.966.2858 www.oculu.com

Oculu is Innovate Media's proprietary video platform and has been serving videos to websites since 2003. We started the business as an online video production company and created a cloud-based online video delivery platform to serve customers who wanted to easily manage and deliver quality to their online viewers. The Oculu platform can be used to serve overlay, embedded, and lightbox video formats to any designated webpage, ad network, or mobile device. The videos launch instantly to stream video content while capturing viewer data for analytics and later evaluation through reporting tools. Oculu delivers videos on 350 customer websites and served over 100 million video plays in 2011 alone.

4. Ooyala, Mountain View, CA 877.366.9252 www.ooyala.com

If you're big on analytics and reporting, Ooyala has really made a commitment to provide clients with these features. They are known for their vigorous reporting. Again, like Brightcove, it can be a bit of overkill. Their dashboard is excellent. Ooyala is one of the bigger OVPs available, and their main focus is publishers who want to serve ads. They have a good reputation for online video management, publishing, analytics, and monetization. Their services and advanced technology provide clients the ability to increase viewer engagement and revenue.

5. Sorenson 360, Carlsbad, CA 888.767.3676 www.sorensonmedia.com

Sorenson Media's main business is video encoding solutions. They are well established in the industry and launched their own OVP a few years ago. It can provide a great platform for video professionals and small to medium-size businesses. The platform can be easily encoded and managed and will deliver good-quality video online to your viewers. This OVP is easy and functional.

6. Vzaar, London, UK 877.831.7110 www.vzaar.com

Vzaar is another great video-hosting choice for businesses. I definitely put them in what I call the middle three (Oculu, Wistia, and Vzaar). Vzaar was developed for professionals and comes preloaded with all the customization, security, and analytical tools needed for online marketers to prove their ROI. Vzaar started as an online platform to help eBay sellers supercharge their sales with video. The company introduced the easiest system eBay sellers had ever used for video. They are based in the United

Kingdom and seem to have a good customer service reputation. I've heard no complaints.

7. Wistia, Somerville, MA 888.494.7980 www.wistia.com

Wistia is a good choice for small to medium-size businesses. In comparison to some of the other midtier OVPs available, their analytics package is robust and provides easy-to-use metrics to support evaluation and redirection of conversions. This OVP also has a tracking platform, by video viewer, that competing services don't have.

About the Author

An online media, marketing, and video expert, John has over 17 years of media experience that includes strategy, sales, marketing, business development, advertising, branding, PR, and affiliate marketing across every medium in the industry. His lifelong career in the media business started right in the middle of video technology's acceleration into homes and businesses. His cable television involvement in the early 1990s and his time with the Yahoo! organization during its early years gave him extensive knowledge of the online advertising and promotion business.

In 2003, John cofounded Innovate Media Group and currently serves as its CEO. He is an evangelist and thought leader for the use of online video in marketing and the promotion of products and services. Since Innovate's founding, John has managed and overseen hundreds of production and video delivery projects for clients that include Canon, Bank of America, HP, Nutrisystem, eHarmony, and Rhapsody.

Under John's leadership, Innovate Media established and launched Oculu.com—a stand-alone online video platform that served over 100 million video plays in 2011 and continues to establish itself as a technology leader in the online video delivery space.

Prior to Innovate, John held positions with such media companies as Lifetime Television and A&E Television. He began his career in the media business selling cable advertising locally for Comcast Cablevision in Southern California.

A native of California, John received his BA in speech from San Diego State University. He resides in Newport Beach with his wife, son, and two daughters.

About Innovate Media Group

Innovate Media Group (Innovate) is a turnkey online video production and delivery company dedicated to the video needs of marketers, agencies, and businesses through its two main properties: Innovate Media and Oculu. Founded in 2003, Innovate first focused on producing web content for consumer electronic, training, and internet-service industries. Soon after, Innovate's domain expanded into technology, providing online video delivery and tracking capabilities to customers.

This technology was specifically developed to solve what clients found most problematic: online video delivery. When clients had a professionally produced, high-quality video ready to present to their customers, they could not find an efficient or effective method to upload that video onto their site.

In 2010, Innovate officially launched this technology as Oculu, a cloud–based, online video platform that seamlessly delivers videos onto a client's site or through social media. Along with ad-free video streaming, Oculu includes a user dashboard, providing users with in-depth tools for analytics, brand awareness, engagement, and loyalty so that marketing decisions can be tracked by each video's performance.

Since its inception, Innovate has produced and overseen hundreds of production and delivery projects for clients including Canon, Bank of America, HP, Symantec, eHarmony, Rhapsody, and many other companies. Oculu has served millions of video plays and continues to establish itself as a technology leader in the online video delivery space.

References

1 Lights, Camera, Action! Text Goes to Video-Based Content

Dave Otten, "Is Video the New Banner Ad," digiday.com, June 2, 2011, http://184–106–158–30.static.cloud-ips.com/stories/is-video-the-new-banner-ad.

Josh Dreller, "The Next Big Things in Video Marketing," imediaconnection.com, March 4, 2011, http://www.imediaconnection.com/printpage/printpage.aspx?id=28593.

Nielsen Wire, "January 2011: Online Video Usage Up 45%," February 11, 2011, http://blog.nielsen.com/nielsenwire/online_mobile/january-2011-online-video-usage-up-45.

Eric Knorr and Galen Gruman, "What Cloud Computing Really Means," infoworld.com, August 7, 2010, http://www.infoworld.com/d/cloud-computing/what-cloud-computing-really-means-031.

Video Uploaded by Bloomberg News, "Walk Says 16,000 Japan Quake Videos Uploaded to YouTube," youtube.com, March 14, 2011, http://www.youtube.com/watch?v=NqKzcddsNiw.

Stan Schroeder, "YouTube Reaches One Billion Views per Day," mashable.com, October 9, 2009, http://mashable.com/2009/10/09/youtube-billion-views.

Craig Wax, "Video Statistics: The Impact of Video," invodo.com, May 11, 2012, http://www.invodo.com/html/resources/video-statistics.

Internet Retailer, "SuperShoes.com Steps Up E-Commerce with Video and Social Elements," May 20, 2009, http://www.internetretailer.com/2009/05/20/supershoes-com-steps-up-e-commerce-with-video-and-social-element.

Real SEO, "Video Demos Increase Sales Conversions at Zappos," http://www.reelseo.com/video-demos-sales-zappos.

L2 Digital Digest, "Boost Traffic and Conversions with Social Integration," March 14, 2011, http://www.l2thinktank.com/l2-origin al-want-more-traffic-go-social/?404=1.

No Author Given, "Online Video and Television Viewing Attitudes and Behaviors," adage.com, May 11, 2012, http://brandedcontent.adage. com/mic/videoadvertising.

Stephanie Flosi, "Online Video Ads Now Reach 50 Percent of Total U.S. Population Each Month," comscore.com, October 21, 2011, http://www.comscore.com/Press_Events/Press_Releases/2011/10 /comScore_Releases_September_2011_U.S._Online_Video_Rankings.

Bill Millar, "Video in the C-Suite: Executives Embrace the Non-Text Web," forbes.com, April 19, 2011, http://images.forbes.com/forbe sinsights/StudyPDFs/Video_in_the_CSuite.pdf.

Marshall McLuhan, "The Gutenberg Galaxy," wikipedia.org, March 12, 2012, http://en.wikipedia.org/wiki/The_Gutenberg_Galaxy.

Author unknown, "Media Influence," http://en.wikipedia.org/wiki /Media_influence.

Henri Lucas, "Visual Communication 2," http://classes.dma.ucla.edu /Spring11/154B.

2 Video in the Media Mix: Where It's Been and Where It's Going

Cynthia Boris, "Nearly 50% of People Surveyed Watch Online Videos Daily," marketingpilgrim.com, February 3, 2011, http://www.marketing pilgrim.com/2011/02/nearly-50-of-people-surveyed-watch-online -videos-daily.html.

Michael Zimbalist, "Out of Digital Chaos, a New Stability for Media," adage.com, January 24, 2011, http://adage.com/article/digitalnext /digital-chaos-a-stability-media/148447.

Author Unknown, "Bing Crosby: His Legendary Years 2," wn.com, 2012, http://wn.com/bing_crosby__his_legendary_years_2.

Author Unknown, "Max Headroom (TV series)," wikia.com, 2012, http://maxheadroom.wikia.com/wiki/Max_Headroom_(TV_series).

Author Unknown, "Max Headroom, Wiki," wiki.glynlyon.com, November 2, 2005, https://wiki.glynlyon.com/wiki/index.php? title=Max_Headroom.

Byron Reeves, "The Benefits of Interactive Online Characters," sitepal. com, 2004, http://www.sitepal.com/pdf/casestudy/Stanford_University _avatar_case_study.pdf.

Author Unknown, "The Videotape that Marked History," seeingisbeliev- ing.ca, October 1, 2002, http://www.seeingisbelieving.ca/handicam /king.

Author Unknown, "Zapruder Film," wikipedia.org, 2012, http://en.wikipedia.org/wiki/Zapruder_film.

Deltaforce5000tm, "Challenger Disaster Live on CNN," youtube.com, July 24, 2007, http://www.youtube.com/watch?v=j4JOjcDFtBE.

Author Unknown, "September 11, 2001—As It Happened—The South Tower Attack," youtube.com, September 11, 2001, http://www.youtube.com/watch?v=1lKZqqSI9-s.

Author unknown, "The Kennedy-Nixon Debates," history.com, 2012, http://www.history.com/topics/kennedy-nixon-debates.

Author Unknown, "Ted Turner," wikipedia.org, 2012, http://en.wikipedia.org/wiki/Ted_Turner.

Harbor Country Bike, "How to Assemble a Multi-Speed Bike/Bicycle," youtube.com, November 15, 2007, http://www.youtube.com/watch?v=8t5quD1hFlQ.

Author unknown, "Purchase Funnel," wikipedia.org, May 10, 2012, http://en.wikipedia.org/wiki/Purchase_funnel.

Mark Robertson, "Using Web Video throughout the Ecommerce Purchase Funnel," slideshare.net, September 2, 2011, http://www.slideshare.net/ReelSEO/using-web-video-throughout-the-ecommerce-purchase-funnel.

3 Participate in the Video Revolution

Fatima D. Lora, "Video Increases Click-Through Rates While Engaging Shoppers," retailtouchpoints.com, November 3, 2011, http://www.retailtouchpoints.com/in-store-insights/1166-video-increases-click-through-rates-while-engaging-shoppers.

Justin Foster, "Top 10 Video Commerce Predictions for 2012—Part 1," videoretailer.org, January 24, 2012, http://videoretailer.org/commerce/top-10-video-commerce-predictions-for-2012-part-1.

Cheryl Jackson-Leafield, "How to Boost Sales, Increase Site Traffic and Generate Leads," pr.com, April 1, 2011, http://www.pr.com/press-release/309923.

Robert Ardell, "Product Tip—How to Videos, Big Train," oculu.com, May 12, 2012, http://www.oculu.com/product-spotlight-how-to-videos.

Stephanie Reese, "Drugstore.com Uses Industry Access to Boost Video Appeal," emarketer.com, May 19, 2011, http://www.emarketer.com/blog/index.php/tag/drugstore-com.

Kevin Rossiter, "Customer Testimonial Video, DVD & Stream," rossiterandco.com, May 12, 2012, http://www.rossiterandco.com/CorporateProducer/CompanyVideoHandbook/CustomerTestimonialVideoDVDStream.htm.

Stephanie Reese, "Interview: Product Videos Hike Sales at Zappos," emarketer.com, June 2, 2011, http://www.emarketer.com/blog/index.php/tag/zappos.

Andrew Tu, "Digital Video Advertising Trends: 2012," breakmedia.com, December 8, 2011, http://cdn.breakmedia.com/wp-content/uploads/2011/12/Video_Study_2012-12-8.pdf.

Ashkan Karbasfrooshan, "The Rise of Video Ad Networks," techcrunch.com, November 19, 2011, http://techcrunch.com/2011/11/19/the-rise-of-video-ad-networks.

Russ Somers, "From eMarketer: Online Video for Retail Gains Sophistication," invodo.com, April 27, 2011, http://www.invodo.com/html/2011/04.

Michelle Renee, "Video File-Sharing Web Sites," ehow.com, April 16, 2012, http://www.ehow.com/list_6685460_video-file_sharing-sites.html.

Author unknown, "File Hosting Service," wikipedia.org, May 11, 2012, http://en.wikipedia.org/wiki/File_hosting_service.

Calfee Czysz, "Impact of Video Sharing on Social and Internal Communication," articlesbase.com, December 22, 2010, http://www.articlesbase.com/internet-marketing-articles/impact-of-video-sharing-on-social-and-internal-communication-3898025.html.

Daisy Whitney, "Personalized TV Tune-In Video Ads Boost Interaction by 40%," mediapost.com, March 28, 2012, http://www.mediapost.com/publications/article/171223/personalized-tv-tune-in-video-ads-boost-interactio.html.

Author Unknown, "Video Overlay," wikipedia.org, May 11, 2012, http://en.wikipedia.org/wiki/Video_overlay.

Sherice Jacob, "Can Product Videos Increase Conversion Rates?" kissmetrics.com, January 16, 2012, http://blog.kissmetrics.com/product-videos-conversion.

Author Unknown, "Popular Video Coupon Codes," retailmenot.com, May 11, 2012, http://www.retailmenot.com/coupons/video.

Diane Williams, "Arbitron Out-of-Home Digital Video Display Study, 2009," arbitron.com, 2009, http://www.arbitron.com/downloads/digital_video_display_study_2009.pdf.

Ryan Lawler, "Report: 80% of Mobile Video Views Happen on Apple Devices," gigaom.com, May 23, 2011, http://gigaom.com/video/apple-dominates-mobile-video.

Dan Ackerman Greenberg, "The Secret Strategies behind Many 'Viral' Videos," techcrunch.com, November 22, 2007, http://techcrunch.com/2007/11/22/the-secret-strategies-behind-many-viral-videos.

Laurel Wentz, "Is Your Detergent Stalking You?" adage.com, July 29, 2010, http://adage.com/article/global-news/marketing-omo-detergent-gps-follow-consumers/145183.

James Nardell, "How Web Video Helped Increase Affiliate Conversions by 80%!" webvideozone.com, 2009, http://www.webvideozone.com/public/321.cfm.

B. L. Ochman, "How to Make a Video Contest Succeed," whatsnextblog.com, July 30, 2008, http://www.whatsnextblog.com/2008/07/how_to_make_a_video_contest_succeed_or_suck.

Monika Jansen, "Boost Your Online Marketing Efforts by Crowdsourcing Videos," networksolutions.com/blog, September 23, 2011, http://www.networksolutions.com/blog/2011/09/boost-your-online-marketing-efforts-by-crowdsourcing-videos.

4 Creating Video: Top Considerations for Production Success

Author Unknown, "The Production Process," mediacollege.com, 2012, http://www.mediacollege.com/glossary/p/production-process.html.

John Cecil, "Increase Conversions—Add Video to Your Website," oculu.com, May 11, 2012, http://www.oculu.com/add-video-to-website-ways-to-increase-conversions.

Matt Cutler, "Why YouTube Viewers Have ADD and How to Stop It," adagec.com, September 30, 2010, http://adage.com/article/digitalnext/marketing-online-video-viewers-quit-30-seconds/146218.

Forrester Consulting, "Watching the Web: How Online Video Engages Audiences," dminnovationforum.com, October 1, 2008, http://www.dminnovationforum.com/media/whitepapers/veoh_forrester_watch.pdf.

Christiaan Harden, "How to Combat Viewer Abandonment in Online Video," steadfast.net, October 11, 2010, http://ip90.208–117–25.static.steadfast.net/business/multimedia/how-to-combat-viewer-abandonment-in-online-video.html.

Bill Sammons, "How to Produce an Effective Video That Works!" watermark-productions.com, May 11, 2012, http://watermark-productions.com/?page_id=5.

John Cecil, "Newsflash: Men Love Online Video Advertising," innovatemedia.com, December 15, 2008, http://www.innovatemedia.com/newsflash-men-love-online-video-advertising.htm.

Corey Kronengold, "Why Pre-Roll Advertising Should Be More Interactive," onlinevideowatch.com, January 4, 2010, http://www.onlinevideowatch.com/why-pre-roll-advertising-should-be-more-interactive.

Jeremy Redgrey, "Pre-Roll Ads Are Re-Purposed TV, Except No One Watches Them," redgreyconcepts.com, June 16, 2010, http://www.redgreyconcepts.com/pre-roll-ads-are-re-purposed-tv-except-no-one-watches-them.

5 Return on Investment (ROI)

Author Unknown, "Eyeblaster Analytics Bulleting Online Video," slide-share.net, November 1, 2009, http://www.slideshare.net/Eyeblaster/eyeblaster-analytics-bulleting-online-video-2939222. "Eyeblaster" is a company that rebranded/changed its name to MediaMind in 2010.

Laura Colona, "A Brand Marketer's Guide to Online Video," collective.com, May 1, 2011, http://collective.com/sites/default/files/Brand%20Marketer's%20Guide%20to%20Video_May2011.pdf.

Dave Kaplan, "Looking at Lift: Inside Online Video Advertising," blog.nielsen.com, April 19, 2010, http://blog.nielsen.com/nielsenwire/online_mobile/looking-at-lift-inside-online-video-advertising.

Lee Odden, "Landing Page Optimization Deep Dive: Interview with Tim Ash," toprankblog.com, April 2010, http://www.toprankblog.com/2010/04/landing-page-optimization-deep-dive-interview-with-tim-ash.

Mike Darnell, "Ecommerce Video A/B Testing—Test Your Intuitions!" treepodia.com, July 19, 2010, http://blog.treepodia.com/2010/07/ecommerce-video-ab-testing-test-your-intuitions.

Author Unknown, "Online Video Analytics," wikipedia.org, August 13, 2011, http://en.wikipedia.org/wiki/Online_video_analytics.

Author Unknown, "Web Metrics 101," opentracker.net, August 4, 2011, http://www.opentracker.net/article/web-metrics-101.

David Strom, "Why You Should Use Video Analytics," readwriteweb.com, June 22, 2011, http://www.readwriteweb.com/enterprise/2011/06/why-you-should-use-video-analy.php.

Jan Ozer, "The 2012 Online Video Platform Buying Guide," onlinevideo.net, March 6, 2012, http://www.onlinevideo.net/2012/03/the-2012-online-video-platform-buying-guide.

Richard van den Boogaard, "Video Marketing Strategy: Hosted Versus Posted Video," reelseo.com, 2010, http://www.reelseo.com/video-marketing-strategy-hosted-versus-posted-video.

Jeremy Scott, "The Week's Best Viral Videos & Marketing Lessons," reelseo.com, 2011, http://www.reelseo.com/weeks-viral-videos-viral-video-marketing-lessons-musical-multitasking.

Chris Wilcox, "Figuring out ROI on Viral Video Clip and Social Media Promoting," webs.com, April 20, 2011, http://juytchris27wilco886.webs.com/apps/blog/show/6786849-identifying-roi-on-viral-video-clip-and-social-media-marketing.

Mark Portu, "Defining ROI for Online Video: A Fluid and Frank Discussion," reelseo.com, 2011, http://www.reelseo.com/defining-roi-video.

6 Delivery

Ron Dawson, "Demand for Video: The Good News and Bad News," daredreamermag.com, January 26, 2012, http://daredreamermag.com/2012/01/26/demand-for-video-the-good-news-and-bad-news.

Jeremy Fain, "Digital Video In-Stream Ad Format Guidelines and Best Practices," iab.net, May 2008, http://www.iab.net/media/file/IAB-Video-Ad-Format-Standards.pdf.

Richard van den Boogaard, "Video Marketing Strategy: Hosted Versus Posted Video," reelseo.com, 2010, http://www.reelseo.com/video-marketing-strategy-hosted-versus-posted-video.

Danny Benefield, "Why Not YouTube?" blog.mydeo.com, February 13, 2012, http://blog.mydeo.com.

Rick Smith, "Best Content Delivery Network to Sell Online Videos: How to Choose," howtosellyourvideos.com, November 23, 2010, http://www.howtosellyourvideos.com/2010/11/best-content-delivery-network-to-sell-online-videos-how-to-choose.

Don Power, "YouTube vs. Vimeo: Which Video Site Is Best for Business?" sproutsocial.com, August 31, 2011, http://sproutsocial.com/insights/2011/08/youtube-vs-vimeo-business.

Dr. Ralph F. Wilson, "The Web Marketing Checklist: 37 Ways to Promote Your Website," wilsonweb.com, April 19, 2011, http://www.wilsonweb.com/articles/checklist.htm.

Douglas Idugboe, "7 Ways to Use YouTube in Your Business," smedio.com, February 2, 2011, http://smedio.com/2011/02/02/7-ways-to-use-youtube-in-your-business.

Christopher S. Penn, "Delivery Strategy Is Separate from Content Strategy," christopherspenn.com, December 2, 2010, http://www.christopherspenn.com/2010/12/delivery-strategy-is-separate-from-content-strategy/#.T7jucuseOrk.

Author Unknown, "Glossary of Online Video Terms," vidcompare.com, 2009, http://www.vidcompare.com/online-video-glossary.php.

Eric Schumacher-Rasmussen, "Editor's Note: Hey Kids, Let's Put on a Show! It's So Crazy, It Just Might Work," streamingmedia.com, June 2009, http://www.streamingmedia.com/Articles/Editorial/Featured-Articles/Editors-Note-Hey-Kids-Lets-Put-on-a-Show!-Its-So-Crazy-It-Just-Might-Work-65492.aspx.

Richard Harrington, "How to Publish Video to the Web," richardharringtonblog.com, April 10, 2012, http://www.richardharringtonblog.com/files/category-web-video.php.

Alexander Dawson, "Mobile Web Design: Best Practices," sixrevisions.com, August 18, 2010, http://sixrevisions.com/web-development/mobile-web-design-best-practices.

Jan Ozer, "Ozer Releases Book: Video Compression for Flash, Apple Devices and HTML5," streaminglearningcenter.com, May 6, 2011, http://www.streaminglearningcenter.com/articles/slc-releases-book-video-compression-for-flash-apple-devices-and-html5.html.

Kim-Mai Cutler, "Brightcove CEO Jeremy Allaire Makes His First Peep after the IPO Quiet Period Ends," techcrunch.com, March 15, 2012, http://techcrunch.com/2012/03/15/brightcove-ceo-jeremy-allaire-makes-his-first-peep-after-the-ipo-quiet-period-ends.

Jeroen Wijering, "HTML5 Video: Not Quite There Yet," longtailvideo.com, May 10, 2010, http://www.longtailvideo.com/blog/11887/html5-video-not-quite-there-yet.

Michael Litt, "Maximize your Video ROI: Understanding What Your Video Analytics Mean," blog.vidyard.com, February 5, 2012, http://blog.vidyard.com/maximize-your-video-roi-understanding-what-yo.

Nathan Evans, "5 Tips for Creating Effective Interactive & Clickable Videos," reelseo.com, 2011, http://www.reelseo.com/tips-creating-great-clickable-videos.

7   Video Production

Jeff Foster, "Choosing the Right Green Screen Materials," provideocoalition.com, November 30, 2011, http://provideocoalition.com/index.php/lightscameraaction/story/choosing_the_right_green_screen_materials.

Anish Patel, "Six Easy Steps to Making Your Video with Revolution Productions," revolution-productions.com, May 3, 2012, http://www.revolution-productions.com/blog.

Renee Casati, "Corporate Video—Working with Audio and Video Talent," xcelusstudios.com, July 22, 2009, http://www.xcelusstudios.com/toddcorbettblog/page/2.

Desiree Sullivan, "Create Your Own Video," gofundme.com, May 1, 2012, http://www.gofundme.com/2012/05/01/create-your-own-video.

Author Unknown, "Digital storytelling," wwwimages.adobe.com, 2008, http://wwwimages.adobe.com/www.adobe.com/content/dam/Adobe/en/education/pdfs/digital-storytelling.pdf.

Denise Atchley, "Digital Storytelling from Soup to Nuts," socialbrite.org, July 21, 2010, http://www.socialbrite.org/2010/07/21/digital-storytelling-from-soup-to-nuts.

Jimm Fox, "Corporate Video Production—What Works Today and Why," onemarketmedia.com, April 3, 2012, http://onemarketmedia.com/blog.

James R. Alburger, "The Art of Voice Acting," scribd.com, 2011, http://www.scribd.com/doc/82161877/The-Art-of-Voice-Acting.

Shawn S. Lealos, "A Beginner's Guide to Film Production," brighthub. com, September 26, 2011, http://www.brighthub.com/multimedia /video/articles/124985.aspx.

Karen Hallford, "Your Best Casting Session," castingworksla.com, 2012, http://www.castingworksla.com/casting_services/casting-services.

Robert G. Nulph, "Tips for Directing Non-Professionals," videomaker. com, April 2009, http://www.videomaker.com/article/14237.

Author Unknown, "3D Animation Studio—What Goes on Behind Those Closed Doors," squidoo.com, 2012, http://www.squidoo .com/3d-animation-studio.

Richard van den Boogaard, "How to Use Royalty Free Music Professionally on YouTube," reelseo.com, October 1, 2011, http://www.reelseo.com /royalty-free-music.

Freddie Wong, "What Is Post Production?" rocketjump.com, March 21, 2012, http://www.rocketjump.com/channels/post-production-what-is-it.

Author Unknown, "Final Cut Pro 5 User Manual," scribd.com, 2005, http://www.scribd.com/doc/29329947/Final-Cut-Pro-User-Manual.

Michael Bluejay, "Getting Video onto Your Website: Web Video Demystified," websitehelpers.com, October 2010, http://websitehelpers .com/video.

Daniel Foster, "How to Create a DIY Green Screen Video Effect," visu-allounge.techsmith.com, May 2, 2012, http://visuallounge.techsmith .com/2012/05/how_to_create_a_diy_green_scre.html.

Author Unknown, "Using Adobe Premiere Pro CS5 in Your Apple Final Cut Pro Workflow," adobe.com, 2010, http://www.adobe.com/content /dam/Adobe/en/products/premiere/pdfs/fcp-users-premiere-pro.pdf.

8 Video SEO—The Science of Getting Seen

Nate Elliot, Forrester Research, "The Easiest Way to a First Page Ranking on Google," January 8, 2009, http://blogs.forrester.com/interactive _marketing/2009/01/the-easiest-way.html.

Natalie Wolchover, "The 5 Most Successful Viral Videos," lifeslittle-mysteries.com, April 25, 2012, http://www.lifeslittlemysteries.com /2390-top-5-viral-videos.html.

General Website Quickstart Guide—Wistia.com, "Setting up Video SEO with Wistia," 2011, http://wistia.com/doc/video-seo.

9 Make Your Videos Social

Lee Rainie, "The Viral Kony 2012 Report," pewinternet.org, March 15, 2012, http://pewinternet.org/Reports/2012/Kony-2012-Video/Main -report.aspx.

Erick Schonfeld, "Facebook Climb to No. 3 Video Site in U.S.," tech-crunch.com, August 22, 2011, http://techcrunch.com/2011/08/22/facebook-3-video-site.

Guest Author, "Share Videos on LinkedIn Using the Slideshare App," linkedin.com/blog, May 6, 2010.

Janko Roettgers, "Intel Takes Moviemaking Social with The Inside Experience," gigaom.com, July 25, 2011, http://gigaom.com/video/the-inside-experience.

Patrick Darling, "Intel and Toshiba Launch Social Media Film Project," newsroom.intel.com, July 11, 2011, http://newsroom.intel.com/community/intel_newsroom/blog/2011/07/11/intel-and-toshiba-launch-social-media-film-project—inside.

Index

DATE DUE	RETURNED
APR 1 5 2015	APR 0 2 2015